The
Colors
of
Money

The Colors
of
Money

Finding Balance, Harmony
and Fullfillment
with Money

Mike Ryan

SUNSTONE
PRESS

SANTA FE

© 2018 byMike Ryan
All Rights Reserved

Sunstone books may be purchased for educational, business, or sales promotional use. For information please write: Special Markets Department, Sunstone Press, P.O. Box 2321, Santa Fe, New Mexico 87504-2321.

Cover photograph by Terri Lilya Keanely

Book and cover design › Vicki Ahl
Body typeface › Californian FB
Printed on acid-free paper
∞
eBook 978-1-61139-539-6

Library of Congress Cataloging-in-Publication Data

Names: Ryan, Mike, 1951- author.
Title: The colors of money : finding balance, harmony and fulfillment with money / by Mike Ryan.
Description: Santa Fe, New Mexico : Sunstone Press, [2018] | Includes bibliographical references.
Identifiers: LCCN 2018000439 (print) | LCCN 2018013056 (ebook) | ISBN 9781611395396 | ISBN 9781632932150 (softcover : alk. paper)
Subjects: LCSH: Money--Religious aspects--Meditations.
Classification: LCC HG220.3 (ebook) | LCC HG220.3 .R93 2018 (print) | DDC 332.4--dc23
LC record available at https://lccn.loc.gov/2018000439

WWW.SUNSTONEPRESS.COM
SUNSTONE PRESS / POST OFFICE BOX 2321 / SANTA FE, NM 87504-2321 /USA
(505) 988-4418 / ORDERS ONLY (800) 243-5644 / FAX (505) 988-1025

For Amatamaji

Contents

Preface / 11

PART I
The Evolution of Money / 13

1 / A Brief History of Money / 23

2 / The Future of Money / 38

3 / Being and Sustainability / 61

PART II
Finding Your MoneyForce

12 / Mental Money, Yellow / 138

13 / The Power of Thought / 148

14 / Soul Money, Violet / 152

15 / The Journey of the Soul / 160

16 / Money in Balance / 165

Preface

Ibegan my career as a Certified Financial Planner® and financial advisor in the early eighties at the beginning of a severe recession.
I retired in 2011 and had experienced four major recessions. I had also
been fortunate to practice during the nineties that saw the United
States experience one of the longest periods of economic growth in
our history. With my clients I felt the fear of loss during the recessions
and the euphoria of seeing investments rise dramatically during the
economic expansions. One of the biggest challenges I faced was not in
determining the best financial strategies using sophisticated techniques
to outperform the market, but in managing the emotions of my clients in
good times and bad. The largest determinate of success in any financial
plan is less the ability of the advisor to outsmart the market, than the
ability of the advisor to manage client expectations and not abandon
the plan during the periods of fear and greed.

This book was first written in 2005 and was self-published in
a very limited edition. This Sunstone Press edition contains some minor
revisions but contains most of the original text. Money is the subject
because during my career I found that as a trusted financial advisor
I was privy to more information about my clients than their family,
friends, and even their minister, priest, rabbi, or imam. When you have
access to someone's finances you will know much about their deepest
feelings and innermost secrets. Money is a common language across all
nations, ethnic groups and religious beliefs. Everyone is involved and
committed to the daily pursuit of making a living. For that very reason
we generally understand that money is the means to our pursuit of happiness and fulfillment. Many will not act as if this is the case and often
make the attainment of wealth as the goal of happiness rather than a
tool to be used in attaining fulfillment through deeper relationships of
family, faith and giving of oneself to a greater good. Over time, with age

and wisdom, the recognition will come of the need to find balance and harmony in our relationship with money and the pursuit of wealth.

Our story begins with a brief history of money and some definitions of what money is. Many are woefully ignorant of how money is created believing for example that the central bank of the United States, The Federal Reserve, is a part of the Federal government. It is actually a private bank owned and controlled by the most powerful private financial institutions in our country. To better understand the functions of money and the effect it has upon our behavior and well-being I will offer stories from my own experience as a financial advisor. We will also explore the deeper aspects of our consciousness, our awareness, as it relates to money. We do this through the teachings of Terri Lilya Keanely who developed a deep sense of inner awareness as a child and spent her entire life in pursuing an understanding of what we would consider spiritual teachings. The teachings used do not contradict any religious beliefs. Terri was herself a Christian but had a deep understanding and respect for all religions and faiths. Terri passed away on October 31, 2015. She is missed. I was fortunate to have the opportunity to study with her for fifteen years. This book is dedicated to her memory in the hope that others may find her knowledge and wisdom as helpful for them as they have been for me.

—Mike Ryan

PART I

The Evolution of Money

Introduction: "Everything Is Every Thing"

> *"Life is the passage of an individual dream, a consciousness, an ego through a cosmic and collective dream. The universe is a dream woven of dreams: the Self alone is awake."*
>
> —Frithjof Schuon[1]

What conflict surrounds us! The duality of creation confronts our entire existence. We are born, grow, learn, teach, remember, forget, love, hate, work, play, sicken, heal, hope, despair, build up, tear down, earn, spend, laugh, cry, worship, desecrate, give, take, inherit, disinherit, sow, reap, honor, debase, do good, do bad, wane, and die. We spend our lives in the pursuit of happiness and fulfillment, the search for wealth in body and soul. Wealth is an elusive state of being, of prosperity, richness, affluence, power, awareness, and contentment, which we think will provide the ways and means for happiness and success.

In his seminal book, *Money and the Meaning of Life,*[2] Jacob Needleman says that hell is a condition that comes from placing value upon what we simply want rather than recognizing and desiring what we truly need. When this happens we are impoverished and deprive our true nature. To experience true wealth—heaven—and embrace infinite richness, we must move beyond the limitation of our wants and open ourselves to our most heartfelt needs.

Money

Although wealth is certainly not measured solely by acquiring and accumulating material goods, the overriding central image and icon of wealth is money. Money is many things. It is a medium of exchange for goods and services and a measure of wealth represented by property, production, display, and conceit, including metals, precious gems, collectables, currency, mortgages and securities, and credit and debit cards, to name a few. It is represented in many forms, but ultimately money is an illusion. Its essence and validity are not self-evident, but are founded solely upon the value or trust imbued upon the asset in question. We engender money with value because we believe it has value and trust that others share that belief. That is the source of the power and force of money. Without that underlying faith and trust there is nothing but empty mass and lost dreams.

Everything is in all things. Nothing positive is disconnected from the whole. What we see, feel, touch, smell, think, imagine, and believe is real, but the complete reality of human experience and consciousness holds much more. The goal of human existence is to develop a complete awareness, understanding, and integration with our true identity and purpose.

In our physical world, wealth is the most important tool human beings have to achieve that goal. It is the nexus of the life matrix, the coalescing force that binds and builds. Money is the language of wealth, the means by which we communicate and express ourselves in our physical form. As with any language, it comes in many types developed over time by and for the people of that age. There is grammar and syntax. We can skillfully express and understand money or find it utterly unintelligible. Money can be as sweet and pure as a Shakespearean sonnet or as base as pornography or hate-filled racist epithets. Just as language is expressed by many voices in many tongues in all fields of endeavor—science, art, business, religion, or politics—so, too, is money fluid throughout the whole of human experience and consciousness.

We are going to explore money. Our intent is not to demonstrate a new get-rich-quick scheme or learn how to exploit other's strengths and weaknesses, but rather to discover money's effect within ourselves. We begin by recognizing that much of our physical life is an illusion. That does not mean it is not real. Often our life is more painfully real than we would like. It is an illusion because what we perceive is not all that is happening. Magic is real. The performers are flesh and blood, and the tricks and illusions conform to the physical laws of the universe, yet does anyone believe that the lady in the revealing costume has indeed been sawed in half? We delight in the mystery and illusion because we know it is not real. We suspend our belief to revel in the mystery of the illusion.

The sun is the source of life on our planet. Without its daily radiation there is no existence. All we see is the reflection of a light spectrum filtered and recognized by our brain. Yet what we see is but a small part of the full force and power of the sunlight we use every day. We do not see the rays of light beyond our perception on both sides of the spectrum high and low, yet we have harnessed their power to our own pursuits in areas such as communication, e.g., radio and TV, and manufacturing items such as microwave ovens. Our inability to see these waves of light has not diminished their reality. Likewise, though we have not developed the faculties and abilities to perceive and understand the fullness of creation, truth does exist.

In the movie, *Defending Your Life*, Albert Brooks played a character that died. In the process of being judged for whether he would continue to higher-level development or be re-born to make up for past mistakes, his defense lawyer told him the purpose of life is to fully develop one's brain. He shared that he used fifty-one percent of his and asked his client what percentage he thought he used. The recently deceased thought a bit, shrugged, and said, "Fifty percent?" His lawyer laughed. "Three percent. We call you 'little brains' behind your backs." The point is, we use a minute portion of our abilities and faculties, and the potential for developing them is indeed beyond our greatest imagination.

Money exists in the real world, in the physical, by the physical, to shape and form the physical. Money also exists in our minds as construct theory and abstract philosophy. Money is fraught with feeling and emotion often dominated by those twin conflicting emotional demons, greed and fear. Money also has soul. Not money itself but the soul energy we project upon money, that energy and power connected to and coming from our soul body that casts on money our highest soul aspirations. Money is the central focus of human energy. Those who wish to understand the meaning of their own life on earth must understand money.

Money Planes

We are going to explore the different levels, or planes, of money consciousness to understand our personal MoneyForce better. MoneyForce is the concerted, conscious, balanced combination of physical, astral (or emotional), mental, and soul energies, powers, and forces we focus to attain wealth. We then consciously apply that wealth to fulfilling our life purpose. The word "level" suggests a hierarchy, which is misleading for our purposes. Each level—physical, astral, mental, and soul—is unique, and each is important and relevant to our complete awareness.

These levels of consciousness are not hierarchical. Each area is uniquely important in contributing to a complete understanding and comfortable relationship with money. The physical level is not inferior to the astral or the mental level, just different, with its own role and purpose.

We will not achieve this awareness by subjugating one money consciousness level to another. Rather, we must balance them and learn how to shift our attention between them to facilitate pursuing wealth and happiness. For that reason we use the term "plane" in this book to describe the different forms of consciousness. We will use plane when we talk about a level of character, existence, and development. In that sense, all planes of existence co-exist equally, at the same time, but at different levels of density and vibration.

Transrational philosopher Ken Wilber in his book *One Taste*,[3] describes the nature of this reality through the use of holons. Holons are individual whole parts that are also part of other whole parts. For example, a cell contains molecules, molecules contain atoms, and atoms contain electrons. An organism contains individual cells, and an entire ecosystem contains individual organisms.

This organization continues throughout the universe with each individual whole part transcending but also including the holons below it on the hierarchy. Cells include molecules, which include atoms, but an atom does not contain a cell. This organization of holons in the physical plane also exists on other levels of existence or consciousness. Spirit is a higher level than soul but includes soul, just as soul is superior to but includes mind, which is greater than but includes emotion. The totality of life comprises all of the unique, independent whole states.

Each plane is separate and unique but they all exist fully, at the same time, in everyone. As we will see, the main problem in relating with and to money comes when these planes become unbalanced and one dominates. We are all familiar with this condition. Think of the nervousness we have during times of emotional stress—"I feel like I'm going to crawl out of my skin"—or the hazy, almost dream-like state we enter when we are so fully immersed in our thoughts that we disengage from all feeling and physical contact.

These occasional lapses into emotional overload or mental reverie are quite normal and necessary. When they become pathological and unbalanced, however, the results can be devastating, destructive, and frightening. The level between extended mental reverie and madness is sometimes a fine line, and the occasional period of high emotion can easily lead to a life of constant emotional anguish. Many times we may feel we have little control over the level and extent of our emotional and mental fluctuations.

We will also learn what colors are associated with the different planes of money consciousness, and how to use color to bring our understanding of money into balance. Color is essential to our lives. Our vision can perceive the colors in the spectrum of sunlight and color ranges exist beyond our visual perception. Without sunlight and the process of photosynthesis there is no life on earth, there is no life for humans. We will explore the meaning of color in the different experiential planes.

During my thirty year career as a practicing Certified Financial Planner®, I met with hundreds of clients. Just as people seldom go to their doctor when they are healthy, my clients would visit me when they had experienced a financial problem or challenge. On the surface, the issue usually appears definite and concrete: "Do I have enough money to retire?" "How can I finance my children's education?" "Can I quit my job and start my own business?"

The real issue, however, is often deeply buried and unspoken: "I'm afraid to retire because I have no other meaning and purpose in my life, no sense of self-identity other than my job." "My son is not meeting my expectations. He doesn't work hard at school, gets terrible grades, does drugs, and plays video games all day. Why should I pay a fortune for him to do the same at college? I feel guilty, though, because I've been conditioned that kids go to college and parents help their kids." "I have to get out of my current job, and this new business deal just came to me from my brother-in-law. It's a sure-fire deal and all my problems will be solved. I don't want to end up like my dad who worked thirty-five years in a dead-end job he hated. It's killing me."

In each instance, the problem was, in part, in the physical issue at hand—retirement, college funding, and business development. But much more, the issue was the imbalance between clients' thoughts and feelings about their particular circumstances. They were unable to think clearly about the situation because they could not detach from the intense emotions they carried. In other instances, their mental defenses were so strongly developed that they were unable to feel any true emotion and connect with their feelings. In each case, the client could not reach a solution until his emotional and mental aspects were more balanced.

Many times the source of this imbalance starts with childhood and the programming we experience during our lives. I remember a wife and husband who were having a difficult time because the husband wanted to start a new business and the wife was blocking him. The wife confessed that because her father lost all his money on a series of failed businesses, her childhood was one of economic deprivation and emotional duress. She witnessed her parent's fight over money and saw her mother succumb to despair. Consequently, she was unable to detach from this psychological state to look rationally at her present condition. Her husband was successful, had a strong business plan and good financing. Yet until she could understand her fear and bring her emotions into line with her rational being, she could not proceed with the plan.

True wealth comes from accumulating sufficient assets to maintain your chosen lifestyle, developing a healthy sense of self-image and self-worth, committing to family and faith, and understanding that giving of yourself is far more rewarding than taking from others. It is not measured in quantity but in quality. During my career I never had a rich client, although my clientele would all fall in the top five percent of wealthy Americans. If asked, I am certain each one would respond in a similar manner: "I'm not rich. Oh, yes, I'm fortunate and blessed to have achieved what I have, but five hundred thousand dollars is certainly not rich. Now if I had a million, I would be rich." The client with one million would say she was not rich but would be if she had five million, and so on. I'm sure at some point true wealth is readily acknowledged, but I did not operate within that level.

This chapter began with the premise that life is a series of contradictions. We indeed have dual natures. We are physical beings striving to exist. We are also spiritual beings with a deep awareness of transcendent reality. Mankind has experienced an ongoing struggle in maintaining a biological existence while attempting to contact and unite with an infinite reality. How can we function in a world that demands the physical necessity of work and social responsibility, while also recognizing and fulfilling the higher potential in all of us?

We cannot turn from either of our natures, but must embrace both, knowing that the answer to our question lies in the intersection of the two spheres. We must embrace and fulfill the totality of our lives to fully experience our highest potential, and this includes serious consideration and acceptance of the role, function, and potential of money in our lives.

Although it often appears that our modern world is bound by darkness and ignorance, there is much to be learned in the absence of light. It is a paradox that often the greatest truths are not revealed on the highest shining mountain peak, but deep in our innermost being, where the greatest mysteries of the universe abide. It takes courage and faith to plunge into these forbidding depths, but deep within lies the heart of wisdom. Our society does not often recognize this need and, unfortunately, rewards shallowness and superfluous endeavor.

Nowhere is the apparent dearth of substance and preponderance of super-ficial shallowness more evident than in the realm of money. Yet there is no other pursuit in this physical realm that occupies more of our time, energy, and focus. We are possessed by our efforts to make a living. Rather than shrink from this fact and retreat into a shroud of illusion and denial in renouncing the material and claiming some noble virtue of poverty and despair, let's embrace our effort and turn from the shallowness so prevalent in our modern folly and dive deep. Everything organic must first grow down before it grows up.

We need to focus our resources and energies toward that goal to achieve our personal and unique quality of wealth in this lifetime. It requires courage, commit-ment, and humility. We must reclaim long-forgotten or lost capacities, abilities, and faculties to have the means to develop and use power, energy, and force to apply to our life purpose.

Every action in life holds the energy and spirit of that person. The money paid in return for work is a repayment, a recognition that energy has been given. Money thus becomes a symbol of our life essence, and as money circulates through-out society, the energy and life force of all humanity unites. When this process is balanced and positive, we all prosper. When it becomes blocked or clouded with negative energy, disharmony is the result. The first is a thing of beauty, the latter a repugnant dissembler.

A sense of wealth is indeed subjective and unique to each individual. What is common to all is the shared relationship we have with money on the four money consciousness planes. In the following chapters, we will look at the history of money to see where we've come from and look at each plane of awareness to see how we can better understand our different money perceptions. We will touch on the different planes of consciousness in which money works in our lives. Each chapter will focus on the nature of the money awareness planes through analysis and anecdotal stories designed to shed light on the particular plane. From these examples we will move to deeper understanding in each area.

Finally, we will present practical techniques for you to awaken your MoneyForce. These simple concentration techniques and practical examples are designed to increase your awareness and understanding of the different money planes.

Lessons and Exercises

Our guide for many of the ideas and practical lessons for achieving our MoneyForce is a wise teacher named Amatamaji, who will answer questions posed by her student, Baraja. The lessons presented by Amatamaji to Baraja express truths about the human condition and are intended neither to endorse nor contradict any religious beliefs. You can find the ideas expressed in many of the world's religions. The exercises as well are not designed to endorse or impede a chosen religious path. In the same manner that physical exercise strengthens the body, these concentration techniques and exercises are designed to support and strengthen your physical, astral, mental, and soul bodies.

This book is not designed to provide you with a better understanding about personal finance or help you develop get-rich-quick schemes. There are many fine books in the former category. As for the latter, my dear old grandma used to say, "If you can't say something good about someone don't say anything."

This book will provide a foundation for you to build a solid relationship with your MoneyForce. You must first secure a strong and secure foundation upon which to build, just as you would when constructing the home of your dreams. We can't promise you will get rich from reading this book, but we can promise that if you follow the ideas and the process and practice the techniques offered, you will begin to awaken your MoneyForce and have the beginnings of a base for whatever financial future your heart desires or your mind conceives. A balanced money consciousness will allow you to use your MoneyForce and equip you to pursue your own quest for true wealth.

1
A Brief History of Money

"The centuries are conspirators against the sanity and majesty of the soul...and history is impertinence and an injury, if it be anything more than a cheerful apologue or parable of my being and becoming."
—Ralph Waldo Emerson[4]

History can be liberating, a beacon directing our personal and collective evolution. It can also be an anchor slowing our journey or, even worse, halting all progress. This chapter identifies several primary themes or generalizations that will put money into context from a level of conscious awareness. What is it about money that motivates, stimulates, activates, eviscerates, and otherwise "turns on" human beings? How has money become such an important and seemingly indispensable aspect of social convention as life evolved on this planet and our species claimed the preeminent position of the biosphere? I'm not sure I have answers to these questions, even if such answers exist or matter, but let's explore what may be found.

Before Money

It is comforting to believe that history is accurate and absolute; that what we are told about an event in the past is indeed precisely what happened. In truth, history is a subjective remembrance clouded with preference and prejudice, dogma and desire. It is possible to determine the absolute truth of any action that occurred in the past, but to do so we would need access to the earth or akashic records. These are the precise records of time the Lords of Karma use to determine their judgments and decisions. This is a difficult undertaking as these records are well hidden. Accessing them requires a high degree of spiritual evolution with finely developed inner sight. Those of us with more mundane capacities, abilities, and faculties must settle for the history we have and hope we can apply the resources we have developed to discriminate between fact and fiction, discern truth from falsehood, and separate reality from illusion.

From a historical perspective, money, as we know it in our modern society and economy, is a relatively recent phenomenon. We can see the precepts of our modern banking system in medieval Europe, but the beginning of modern money commences with the founding of the Bank of England in 1694. Our sense of recorded history gets sketchy when we get much past 4,000 B.C. Although anthropologists continue to push back the date of the origin of the species, these ancient possible predecessors bear little resemblance to anyone we might meet on the street. We can be more confident that by about 100,000 B.C. Homo sapiens, our species, emerged in southern Africa. These anatomically modern humans settled in northern Europe between 35,000 B.C. and 12,000 B.C. during the Upper Paleolithic period.

As climatic changes brought warmer temperatures, the ice sheets covering much of the northern hemisphere receded, allowing human expansion into these once inhospitable lands. The melting ice released water into the atmosphere, and the increased rainfall turned former deserts into rich farmland, spurring agricultural development during the Agricultural Revolution, 10,000 to 4,000 B.C. As former hunter-gatherer societies turned to farming for sustenance, more permanent villages developed. The transition from a society of hunter-gatherers to a village-centered agricultural economy is perhaps the most important influence on the development of money. It is estimated that in 15,000 B.C. the entire world population of ten million people were hunter-gathers. By 1,500 B.C. the world population had grown to 350 million people with only one percent existing as hunter-gathers, who were located primarily in the northern half of North America and Australia, landmasses separated geographically from the rest of the world's populations.

In *The Way of Animal Powers*,[5] Joseph Campbell observes that man is a beast of prey, a hunter. Hunters of all species are intimately involved with death both as hunter and hunted. Yet unlike other animals that exist by preying on others, man is unique. At what point in our evolution from lower levels of creation did we first become aware of our unique place among all living things?

From the moment man recognized death, he also opened the possibility for achieving a level of consciousness apparently unavailable to other animals. Other animals live in the moment, seeing death around them but unaware of its meaning. Man alone becomes old with full awareness of his mortality.

Hunter-gathers have no need for money, certainly not money in the modern sense. They have no need for currency, because there is no transactional commerce in their society. Although physically demanding, a hunter-gather's life is not complicated. A typical day might go something like this: The men hunt with varying degrees of success, and when sufficient game has or has not been slaughtered, they return to the small tribe to spend the rest of the day and night relaxing, smoking, drinking, dancing, organizing the religious activities of the clan, and making preparations for whatever military defense or offense is determined necessary for the well-being of the tribe. The women and children are the gatherers and spend considerably more time, effort, and energy gathering edible roots, plants, and firewood, preparing the daily meal, and maintaining the family and its clothing and shelter. When the game or local flora grows scarce the clan moves to follow the game and find new growth.

Whereas money is useless to these people, what appears indispensable is a sense of living in harmony with the essentials of their survival, the land, the prey, and their perception of their own mortality, their personal involvement in the endless cycle of birth and death. Some of the earliest records we have of these people are cave paintings that indicate a heightened awareness of the almost sacred nature of the hunt and female figures depicting the fecundity of the earth. For Stone Age man, the balance between survival and starvation was a daily effort. Probably the closest we can come to having a perception of the reciprocal value we put on money is the relationship the hunter-gathers had with their prey and the earth. The hunt, ever reverent of game and dependent on weapons, was their money. Seasonal cycles with the resulting dearth or abundance were their credit cards. The sun's rising and the moon and stars' passage were their bank deposits.

As we trace the development of money through history, we will come back to these ancient origins. We shall see that the basic economic unit has always been the family and the household, and that survival has depended on a division of labor between the paternal—hunter—and the maternal—gatherer. This was coupled with special emphasis on the place of shelter, dependence on harmony with nature, and awareness of a transcendent reality demonstrated in recognizing our mortality.

Although prehistoric culture clearly had no use for money, it would be a mistake to draw the conclusion that the use and intricacy of money economies developed linearly as societies developed and grew more complex. Some highly developed cultures did not use money as the basis for their economy—most notably ancient Egypt and the medieval feudal manor system.

These cultures are far removed both in time and social structure from prehistoric hunter-gatherer societies, but they all share a common structure: the economic foundation of each is the household and the social organization is well defined and rigidly enforced. To put it another way, the well-being of the collective is placed before the personal interests of the individual.

To say that ancient Egypt did not have money is a bit misleading. They did not use coinage or other forms of currency as we know it, but they used metals as a basis of exchange to a limited extent, and grain stores were their primary form of monetary value and exchange.

In *The Story of Money*,[6] Norman Angell describes developed civilizations that have existed without money, including ancient Egypt and the medieval feudal estates. In their day-to-day operations, there was no need for money. The basic social unit was the household, and hierarchy and division of labor in the social classes was rigid and strictly controlled. An economy based upon the needs of the collective rather than the individual has little need for money. As individual freedom increases in a civilization, so does the need for a money economy.

Economists define money as anything that can be exchanged for goods and services, received without assay or special quality test, and received with no reference to the credit of the one offering payment. Angell describes the functions of money as a medium of exchange, a standard of deferred payment, and a measured store of value.

History has recorded periods of moneyless civilizations longer than moneyed, which is hard to imagine in a society preoccupied and obsessed with money such as ours. It often appears that the examples of a money economy are aberrations in a moneyless continuum. As we shall see, coinage was introduced relatively late in ancient Greece and the resultant social and economic problems coincided with the decline of that civilization. Likewise, the decline of Rome has been attributed by some historians as much to the instability of its monetary policy as to any social or moral causes.

First Money

Coins were certainly not the first money. Long before coinage was introduced, commodities such as grain, shells, stones, feathers, beads, animal hides, cattle, and agricultural implements functioned as money, rather than simply as a means of barter. Later, metals in the form of ingots or rods served as money. When the ingots were stamped for weight or quality and the size decreased, coins resulted.

The earliest literary works in western civilization are Homer's *Iliad* and *Odyssey*. They depict an agrarian economy of independent feudal city-states dominated by autocratic warrior kings. There is neither money nor any cultural values that required money. This was a heroic age where the utmost esteem and virtue was placed upon the warrior hero. No merchant class, trade, markets, or money existed.

In the *Iliad*, there is a passage where the Greek, Diomedes, makes fun of the Trojan, Glaucus, for the uneven exchange of armor worth nine oxen for armor worth one hundred. It is not that cattle were actually used as currency, but rather as a measure of value. We may compare our modern use of paper currency, which was formerly backed by either gold or silver and currently backed by the full faith of the issuing government. We also have more recent examples of a commodity being used as a measure of value. In pre-revolutionary colonial America, tobacco served a similar function in Virginia, wool in Rhode Island, rice in South Carolina, and sugar, rum, molasses, and skins in other areas.

It is commonly believed that the first coins originated in Lydia, a kingdom in Asia Minor, primarily from reference in Herodotus' Histories. Herodotus makes the rather wry observation that apart from prostituting their daughters without exception, the Lydians had a lifestyle quite similar to the Greeks and were the first people to use coins in retail trade. Numismatists support Lydia as the origin of coinage because the earliest coins we have are Lydian. They are not coins as we would know them, but more like oval ingots stamped on one side. They were made of electrum, a naturally occurring amalgam of gold and silver. By the time of Croesus, from whence came the phrase "rich as Croesus," pure gold and, more often, silver had replaced electrum because the amalgam was too easily debased. This introduces us to a constant theme we shall see with certain regularity: the trend for the debasement of coins. As new coins were introduced with less gold, people hoarded the old coins and used the new, less valuable coins—thus Gresham's law that bad money will always drive out good.

Money as an Archetype

You have now seen an economic definition of money and the different functions of money, but money has another aspect. It is not just a physical medium of exchange, but also serves an archetypal function within the human psyche.

Throughout history, people have spent the majority of their existence in a mortal struggle to obtain food and shelter. The affluent middle class that emerged in western societies during the past one hundred years is an anomaly. Even today, the majority of the planet's inhabitants exists in utter poverty and treads a thin line of existence. We have discussed among hunter-gathers the importance of the hunt and the symbiotic relationship between hunters and the hunted. In these societies, the family unit was essential to survival with each member providing a required function, and the home, with its fire and hearth, the central icon of the household. In our modern world, where the nuclear family is a vestige, consuming food has become a meaningless, simple satiation of hunger or the substitute for other unfulfilled desires.

In his wonderful book, *The Secret Life of Money,*[7] Tad Crawford explains the archetypal nature of money as an inherited pattern or mode of thought or behavior developed by experience and shared unconsciously by individuals within a group. It is an intimate part of human exchange and relationship. As we become more aware of money, we become more aware of ourselves.

Money is a strong symbol in our lives because it is an archetype. The basic human need for food and shelter drives the daily efforts of most people. The early history of money was closely tied to the family, the basic social institution, and the functions of the family—the common meal and the hearth. The shared meal is at the core of money's symbolic meaning. Thus money's common thread through the generations is humanity's need for survival and relationship.

In ancient societies, the daily struggle for survival elevated food sharing to the level of sacred ritual. Money symbolized the survival of the individual spirit, the soul, because it was associated with family survival. The Greek philosopher-warrior, Xenophon, first introduced the word oikonomikos—economics—which meant the skill needed in managing a household. In his book, Economics, he detailed practical information regarding the management of a home, which in ancient Greece would have been the sole domain of women.

Economics as an area of household management in Greece coincided with the country's market economy development. The introduction of coinage provided the necessary exchange medium for effective and efficient open market operation. Many of the other older societies such as Egypt and Persia had economies based on rigid tribute systems and strict totalitarian control. Greece, composed of decentralized, independent city-states, was the first to recognize the advantage open markets provided for commerce and wealth creation. Money was the system's essential fuel. Fortunately for the Greeks, this cultural development coincided with the discovery of significant silver deposits there.

A market economy does more than provide the means for wealth creation. It is the prime venue for social and cultural diversification. When societies exchange goods and money changes hands, they exchange cultural and social ideas as well. In *The History of Money*,[8] Jack Weatherford observes that money has the unique ability to function as metaphor for a whole range of human expression and desire. Wherever money goes, it creates a market for goods and for a full range of ideas—political, religious, social, and personal. Cities grew and human relationships expanded with money's advent.

The origin of the word money comes from the Latin monetta, which was an aspect of the goddess Juno. In the Greco-Roman pantheon, the gods were human archetypes. They represented the collective unconscious. The gods were a family with a father, Zeus (Jupiter), and a mother, Hera (Juno). Juno had several feminine aspects. As Juno Regina, she ruled as queen of the gods. Juno Pronuba oversaw marriage. Juno Lucina protected pregnant women. And Juno Sospita served as a sort of divine midwife during labor and childbirth.

Juno was Rome's mother goddess and fertility goddess. The month of June, the beginning of the growing season and a favored month for marriage, was named after her. As protector of women, who were considered the guardians of the family and the household, Juno assumed the role of guardian of the state. According to Roman legend, in the fourth century B.C., alarmed geese honking around Juno's temple alerted the Romans to an impending attack from the Gauls, and the city was saved. In recognition, the goddess was given the name Juno Monetta, from the Latin monere—to warn.

The temple of Juno Monetta served as the state mint where money was coined. In this sense, money flow is linked to the earth goddess' fertility. The image that immediately comes to mind is Liberty, a regular fixture on U.S. coins, especially our gold coins and the Liberty fifty-cent piece. Historians depicted Juno Monetta as a full-figured woman, neither young nor old, with flowing hair and radiant in her fecundity. She stands with infants in each arm and is adorned with the fruits of the harvest. All around her stand animals eager to receive her fertile gifts. A constant source of gold and silver coins flows at her feet. She is everything abundant, nourishing, and life-giving, a physical source of divine, infinite power. Other historians have noted the relationship between money and the goddess, stating the earliest currencies—commodities such as shells, grains, cattle, and gold—were all surrogates of the Great Mother.

Egyptians used barley as a currency, and they imbued their money with an almost magical divine attribution by identifying the source of power and influence of these commodities as the Great Mother. In the Pharaohs' tombs, figures of the god, Osiris, composed of germinating barley grains, were placed to imbue the dead Pharaoh with the Great Mother's life-giving properties.

When gold, the most precious and immutable of all metals became the basis for money, it too carried a divine identity. It is as if using the metal to transact daily business brings the gods' divine life to earth. Therefore, in money there is fecundity and wealth, but the Greeks and Romans also recognized the need for caution, measurement, and mental clarity when dealing with money.

Money in the Middle

The Military Order of the Knights of the Temple of Solomon was founded in 1118 by the first crusaders, who remained in the holy land to protect pilgrims to Christendom's sacred shrines. The Templars, through special dispensation from the papacy, soon became one of the largest, wealthiest, and most powerful forces in medieval Europe. The Templars created the most powerful international financial system of the time, which lasted until 1310 when King Phillip IV of France and Pope Clement V abolished the order through a gruesome purge and execution of its leaders.

We have previously noted how, following the decline of the Roman Empire, Europe entered a period where the highly organized structure of a feudal manor society required little need for money. It could be said the event that signaled the beginning of the end of feudal society was the call to crusade by Pope Urban II in 1095. The first crusade had a catalyzing effect on the people of Europe, from the nobles to the peasants, and the renewed contact with the East introduced the beginning of the great mercantile empires that would flourish throughout the middle and late middle ages, terminating with Spain's boom and bust in the sixteenth century.

Much of the Templars' wealth came from their extensive land holdings and their banking system. As a military religious order, the Templars not only had fortified castles throughout the world, but also the military might to defend those holdings. In an era when travel of any sort was fraught with danger, traveling with large amounts of gold was particularly hazardous. The Templars devised a deposit system where merchants could leave money in one Templar stronghold, travel to their destination, and receive payment from the local Templar castle. The Templars charged a fee for the transaction and took a profit from the exchange rate between currencies.

In addition to these currency transactions, the Templars provided much of the financing desperately required in a time of almost constant war, although they were less a bank than a royal credit union lending to royalty and the papacy. The kings of Europe also required immense sums to protect their feudal holdings and borrowed heavily from the Templars. It is this increased wealth and power over pope and king alike that led to the Templars' demise.

The banking families of Venice, Genoa, and Florence filled the gap formed when the Templar system collapsed. The Italians greatly expanded the concept of banking and its market, extending credit to the rising merchant class as well as the aristocracy and the church. Like the Templars, the renaissance bankers of Italy faced a major obstacle in developing their business: the Christian prohibition against usury. "Thou shalt not give him thy money upon usury, nor lend thy victuals for increase,"(The Bible, Leviticus 25:36-37) and "He that hath given in usury and hath taken increase: shall he live? He shall not live: he hath done all these abominations; he shall surely die, his blood shall be upon him."(The Bible, Ezekiel 18:13) Whereas the Templars finessed this proscription by not lending money but charging a fee for a service, the Italians developed the basics of modern banking.

The Italian merchant families traded bills of exchange rather than making loans. A merchant who needed money went to a banker in Italy, received the required money in cash, and signed a bill of exchange requiring payment of a slightly higher amount than borrowed, to be paid in the currency of another country in which the merchant was doing business. The lending banker also received a fee for the currency exchange. The merchant then set up his table, or banco, to do business in the city's central market.

The new financial centers of Florence and Venice developed their own currency, the florin and ducat, as they emerged and grew wealthy. The Venetian ducat (from the Latin ducere, to lead) was introduced in 1284 and remained in circulation for five hundred years until the fall of the Republic of Venice in 1797. That the ducat remained unchanged in purity is even more amazing. Contrast that with ancient Rome where, over the span of two hundred years (A.D. 65–268), the silver content of the denarius was cut from one hundred percent to less than five percent.

The creation of a true banking system invigorated the economy of renaissance Europe. For example, let's say a merchant in Venice wished to do business with someone in Paris. Transporting gold across the countryside was perilous. To manage the risk, the Venetians created an ingenious device. The merchant would deposit one hundred gold ducats with his banker in Venice. The banker would then issue a bill of exchange to the merchant for the value of one hundred gold ducats, which the merchant could use to transact business in Paris. The bank in Venice would then lend the one hundred ducats to someone else, thus creating money. The flow of the original one hundred gold ducats through the system created several hundred gold ducats, increasing liquidity and facilitating the flow of commerce. The process seemed almost magical in its ability to generate money.

Magic indeed and like magic it required a suspension of belief and complete trust in the skill, talent, and dexterity of the magician. Through the magic of leverage, the original one hundred ducats was transformed into several hundred ducats of purchasing power, but the success of the entire enterprise depended on all participants' total trust in each others' word and ability to make good on the debt when payment was required.

The Renaissance not only introduced the modern banking system, but also other important innovations in the history of money. Double-entry bookkeeping, which greatly improved the merchant's ability to keep track of accounts, was possibly the most important and enduring of these. Leonardo Fibonacci introduced Arabic numerals in 1202. This allowed merchants to compute without an abacus and, throughout the fifteenth and sixteenth centuries, great strides were made in the field of mathematics, culminating with the publication by Isaac Newton in 1686 of Principia Mathematica.

Perhaps the most dramatic monetary event of the late middle ages was Spain and Portugal's conquest of Mexico and South America and the effect on their economies of the gold and silver mined in those countries. From the first conquest until 1800, it is estimated that between 145,000 and 165,000 tons of silver and almost 3,000 tons of gold were shipped. At a per ounce price of four hundred dollars for gold and six dollars for silver, that would amount to an increase in the money supply, in current dollars, of over seven trillion dollars over the three centuries. The increase was unprecedented for that time and those economies.

The effect was not surprising. The traditional definition of inflation is "too much money chasing too few goods and services." This was certainly the case in Spain, where prices rose four hundred percent between 1500 and 1600. The Spanish found themselves in the unique position of being cash rich, yet with little real wealth because their economy did not use the inflow of money to increase production. They produced few goods of their own, imported extensively, and used their huge gold and silver reserves to borrow. The end result was national bankruptcy. As we shall see, this tendency towards inflation and the resulting economic instability this creates continues into our era.

Modern Money

The four major modern monetary developments are: paper money, electronic money, abandonment of the gold system, and national banks independent of their respective governments. Glyn Davies, in his detailed *A History of Money*,[9] notes that the modern era was launched through the influence of gunpowder, the mariner's compass, and the printing press. Without the invention of printing, we would not have money as we know it nor would we be subject to the problems that arise when money is printed without restraint.

The world's first paper money originated in China, appropriately, since the Chinese invented paper. What is surprising is that the first large-scale economic application of paper money occurred during the Mongol empire. The Mongols have long carried the image of bloodthirsty marauding savages. In addition to their unsurpassed ruthlessness, they were highly successful administrators of a multicultural empire. Under the Mongols, China became part of a vast empire that extended from Korea to the Danube. To standardize currency throughout Asia, the Mongols adopted China's paper money. Marco Polo, who lived in China from 1275 to 1292, wrote in his Travels "The coinage of this paper money is authenticated with as much form and ceremony as if it were of pure gold or silver."

It is said that the United States is primarily motivated by desire for the almighty dollar. The word dollar originates from the Bohemian thaler, which became the most widely distributed coin of the Austro-Hungarian Empire. The United States adopted the dollar as a statement of anti-English or anti-authoritarian bias, because British fiscal policy forbade the exportation of specie, even to its own colonies. Due to the proximity of Mexico and the economic strength of Spain, the most common coin in the British colonies was the so-called pillar dollar, named for the depicted Pillars of Hercules, the ancient name for the strait connecting Spain and Morocco that bore the inscription plus ultra (more beyond), signifying the discovery of America.

Paper money is fragile physically and emotionally, for those who use it. It is prone to counterfeit and vulnerable to extreme swings of inflation and deflation. Whereas hyperinflation in Germany during the twenties exists as a vague historical footnote to us, Peter Angell's reports of excerpts from the _London Times_ brings the events in Europe to life:

> May 16 1923 – The dollar went to 46,000 today. Foodstuffs have gone up considerable in price.
>
> June 1 – The dollar has reached 77,000 marks. It has come as a great shock to a great many Germans to realize that their currency is now in a worse plight than that of Austria, worse even than that of Poland, and the only one worse than theirs is that of Soviet Russia.
>
> June 10 – Yesterday the mark touched 88,000 to the dollar. Prices in the retail shops are rising literally "while you wait."
>
> June 18 – Today the price of the dollar advanced from 120,000 to 152,000.
>
> July 25 – It is hard to know what to say or think with conditions moving as they are. It is like being caught in a typhoon. One holds on and hopes for the best.

The scope of the inflationary spiral challenges the imagination. From a baseline of 100 in 1913, the price index rose from 147,479 in December 1922 to 75,570 trillion in November 1923.

The specter of economic chaos hovers over financial markets in spite of the mitigating effects on runaway inflation in developed economies through strengthened national banks, recognition of past errors, and creation of lenders of last resort such as the IMF and the World Bank. In August 1998 deflationary conditions in Asia threatened to engulf South America and the U.S. economy was extremely vulnerable. The intervention of U. S. Treasury Secretary Robert Rubin, creative financing by the International Monetary Fund (IMF), and the acquiescence of the Federal Reserve Board averted a potential calamity. Yet the potential for disaster is inherent in the system.

Robert Rubin, a master of financial markets from his trading days on Wall Street, recognized during the height of the financial crisis the danger should it spread. He elicited the banking support of the IMF, which had at first balked by claiming to be tapped out from bailing out Russia. Rubin reminded the IMF that they set their own reserve requirements, which they quietly amended, thus freeing up the necessary capital. The money center banks were definitely on board because they were on the hook for the greatest losses should the system collapse. The hitch was the Federal Reserve, whose role would be to cut interest rates. Although the chairman was in tow, there was one obstinate governor who insisted on holding firm on the Fed's stance in keeping rates high to combat possible inflation. At the meeting in Washington all the parties sat as Rubin presented the plan, and one by one the various parties agreed to the scheme. All eyes were on the recalcitrant fed governor who sat in stony silence.

Following the meeting an old friend who once worked for this particular gentleman went up and asked, "Why didn't you object to the Fed's lowering interest rates?" The man looked him in the eye and replied, "Jim, I was having a liquidity crisis of my own," thus eradicating the belief those of us uninitiated in the world of high finance embrace—that the world's financial affairs are determined with rational certainty. Sometimes the future course is determined as much by a strained bladder as by the eager machinations of all the king's men.

Electronic derivatives are another recent development in the history of money. As the name implies, the value of the security is derived from another source. For example, the S&P 500 Index represents a market basket of five hundred stocks of large, well-known companies. The index exists as a market performance benchmark, but can be replicated by purchasing its underlying securities. An option to buy or sell the value of the S&P 500 derives solely from the value of the underlying index.

Options and their cousin, financial futures, have long played an important role in managing market risks, especially in commodity markets. Take, for example, a corn farmer and the cornflake manufacturer. The farmer determines a price that will provide him with sufficient profit from the sale of the corn crop. He does not know what the price will be at the time of harvest and is open to that risk. Conversely, the cereal producer can price the cost of corn in his product in advance. Each side has a strong incentive to enter into a future contract to deliver and purchase the corn crop at a specified price to maintain stability at each end of production. In the interim, the futures contract may be bought and sold many times as speculators bet on whether the market price of the commodity at delivery will be higher or lower than the contract price.

The ringer in this system is the introduction of borrowing, or leverage. If I purchase a security and put up only fifty percent of my own money while borrowing the balance, I have leveraged my potential profit or loss. A stock purchased for ten dollars that rises in price fifty percent to fifteen dollars will result in a profit to me of one hundred percent (less the interest I pay for using the borrowed money). In contrast, if the stock goes down by fifty percent, I lose all of my original investment plus the interest on the loan. If I believe the price of the security will go up, I want to own the stock and will take a long position. If I think the price will go down, I will sell the security short by borrowing the stock, selling it, and replacing it to the lender in the future at a lower price.

This ability to bet on future prices by going long (buying) or short (selling) securities is called hedging, because we can attempt to manage the risk of fluctuating prices by buying securities we think are undervalued and selling securities we believe are overvalued.

Pools of money managed in this fashion are called hedge funds and are perhaps the most sophisticated form of money yet invented. Simply put, hedge funds are an investment where the manager has the ability to invest both long (betting on higher prices) and short (betting the security will go down in price). By combining these positions, a manager can theoretically reduce risk. This is the structure, but the real kicker comes with using leverage. Bill Gross, manager of the PIMCO family of mutual funds, says hedge funds are unregulated banks. Just as banks make money on the spread between the interest they pay for deposits, and the interest they charge for loans, hedge funds leverage their capital in a similar manner.

If I want to buy a stock, I can purchase it for cash with no leverage or buy it on margin from my broker and put up half the value of the stock plus pay the broker the going interest rate. In contrast, the hedge fund manager puts up only two to four percent in cash and borrows the other ninety-eight percent and pays interest on this at a much lower percentage. There is little transparency—the ability to see what transactions take place—and no regulatory oversight. The manager has the ability to borrow and leverage the investment, all in hopes of huge profits. This may be fine when all works as planned, but as soon as the deal goes south the repercussions of unregulated, secretive, overly leveraged money-making are catastrophic on a world economic system unable to support the crisis. As more and more investors funnel money into hedge funds in the hope of great profits, the likelihood of hedge fund managers finding inefficiencies to exploit diminishes with the overcapacity, and the likelihood for severe stress on the system increases.

I wrote the first edition of this book in 2005 before the financial crisis of 2008. In hindsight we now see the impact to a world financial system that may occur when the pursuit of profit, unconstrained by government or industry oversight, is permitted. Although there have been some restraints put in place to increase the liquidity and financial stability of large banks and other financial institutions, there are many who feel that these are not of enough substance to prevent another financial meltdown from occurring in the future.

2
The Future of Money

"The device used to create the scarcity indispensable for a bank-debt system to function involves having people compete for the money that has not been created, and penalizes them with bankruptcy whenever they do not succeed. The current monetary system obliges us to incur debt collectively, and to compete with others in the community, just to obtain the means to perform exchanges between us. No wonder 'it is a tough world out there,' and Darwin's observation of the 'survival of the fittest' was so readily accepted as self-evident truth by the 18th century English, as well as by any societies that have accepted, without question, the premise of the money system that they designed, such as we have today."
—Bernard Lietaer[10]

What is money's role in this great new age? Perhaps our insight into what money will become is to look at what money has been and imagine or visualize how it may be transformed. In Chapter 1 we looked at how money developed during the course of civilization. We noted that our present money system has its foundation in the late seventeenth century with the founding of the Bank of England, and our contemporary system began in 1971 when President Nixon removed the dollar from the gold standard. Our present credit-based monetary system is about three hundred years old, forty-five in its most current iteration. If we accept the origin of historical civilization and the first forms of money as around 3000 B.C., then the lifetime of our current monetary system comprises only six percent of the entire period of money's existence. More importantly, our present system, based entirely on fiat currency or the belief that the dollar has value simply because the U.S. government says it does, comprises a mere 0.6 percent of money's history.

Historically, fiat currency is unstable because of the transitory nature of political systems. People demanded there be something of intrinsic perceived value to back the currency in use, normally either agricultural commodities or precious metals, with gold as the standard of choice. Today there is no standard of value for the entire world credit system, save the belief in the stability and credit of the United States. National governments, however, regardless of their power, exist on a tenuous framework. If there is any natural rule of politics, it is that every world power from the ancient Egyptians, to the Greek Empire of Alexander, the Romans, the Mongol Horde, Napoleonic France, the Ottoman Empire, the British Empire, and, finally, the United States will fall from their lofty heights. What we don't know is how the current superpower will recede, when that will occur, and the effect of this eclipse on the world monetary system.

What Is Money?

Money may be defined as anything that can be exchanged for goods and services and received without any quality test and with no reference to the credit of the one offering payment. It functions as a medium of exchange, a standard of deferred payment, and a measured store of value. Like the three blind men describing the elephant based on the part they were touching, so money systems are identified and implemented by different definitions and perceived functions of money. Unlike the solid elephant, money is mercurial and ever changing. In one moment it serves as a store of value and requires the necessary attributes to fill that role. Then, in an instant, it must become a medium of exchange, which may require functions not at all compatible with those that best fit its purpose as a store of value. Traditionally, when the desire is to protect the value of money, we have used commodities such as cattle, beads, wheat, silver, or the most favored, gold. Money backed by a commodity may indeed provide the most stable measurement for its value. Yet all commodities have the weakness inherent in their physical limitations. They are finite, and must be produced, transported, and stored. At each stage they are vulnerable to human manipulation. The history of gold-backed money is full of examples of inflation when gold became too plentiful, or deflation when gold was too scarce. In both cases, market functions both scrupulous and immoral can manipulate the commodity.

In contrast, when money becomes a medium of exchange, the goal is to facilitate the transfer of goods and services through a mechanism where both parties experience an equitable and fair exchange. All transactions beyond direct barter create credit. When I sell you a tangible good or service and receive monetary payment, credit has been extended in the transaction. I have trust in the soundness of the credit represented in the money. Money is credit. The system requires a delicate balance between the amount of money in circulation and the available production of goods and services. Too much money relative to the supply and price inflation will occur. Too little, and prices will fall for lack of available credit.

Money is not wealth, although it may be confused as wealth because it is so integrated into wealth creation. Wealth is the outcome of valued productivity created solely through the intervention of the unlimited potential of human ingenuity, creativity, compassion, and love. There is nothing intrinsic to wealth. People work land to provide sustenance and raw materials, which provides the time and means for other production. These products in turn enable comfort and foster social, cultural, scientific, and economic development. Wealth is created because we value this process of enablement and evolutionary development.

Wealth is abstract and often arbitrary. In seventeenth century Holland, owners of prized tulip bulbs possessed untold wealth for a brief time. When reason again prevailed, these burghers had only their pretty flowers to treasure. Value is best determined in open markets where the ebb and flow of supply and demand provides the best opportunity to measure the price of any given good or service in that place and time. It is not a perfect measure because the participants are people, and people posses a divine soul connection as well as human attributes and are capable of actions respective of each. We may soar to the highest realms of love, honesty, and compassion or sink into the lowest morass of malignancy, mendacity, and hostility.

This is why we have always recognized that money has a deep moral aspect. We may even aspire to a higher spiritual awareness of money. Think of how you use money. For most of us it does not function as a store of value. We store those assets in the form of means of wealth production such as land, real estate, business, and physical and intellectual property, or in securities of wealth-producing capital assets including equity and debt. Most of us are not involved in barter economies, and we use money for commercial transactions whenever we want to buy something. Money is credit. Credit exists because of mutual trust. Trust is founded in the moral precept that we treat others in the manner in which we would like to be treated. This conviction exists in both religious and non-religious systems of morality.

Societies have from earliest times recognized the synergy between moral values and money. In Rome money was created in the temple of Juno Monetta and controlled under the auspices of the head of the church, the Pontifus Maximus. Julius Caesar combined his role as head of the church with head of state, and this established a connection between money and the state that continues to this day. Although we profess a connection when we print the motto "In God We Trust" on our currency, we do not consciously understand the implications of this deep connection between money and the highest aspirations of human morality. We are a secular society dedicated to individual freedom and separation of church and state, yet we have rooted deep within our collective unconscious an understanding of the absolute imperative for a moral foundation in our relationship with money. When trust is lost, money fails.

Trust is built upon actions, but ultimately depends upon a leap of faith. Actions can be duplicitous or mitigated through complex machinations meant to perpetuate the appearance of moral behavior where none exists. The financial crisis of 2008 provides an excellent example of this. Corruption comes in shades from grey to black. When the public loses faith in its institutions, whether government or commercial, no money system can be stable. When trust is lost, it takes a very long time to reestablish. Dante places those who betray trust—Brutus and Judas—in the deepest bowels of hell. Betrayal of the money trust is a transgression of the commonwealth, the mutual assets of the people. In a democracy, which is government of the people, by the people, and for the people, this amounts to high treason. Redemption requires confession and restitution. Heartfelt confession signifies recognition of wrongdoing, contrition, and a sincere desire for transformation. Only then is there a foundation for a renewal of trust.

How Does Money Work?

Money is both a store of value and a medium of exchange. Money is credit. When credit is extended, debt is created at the same time. Debt is the shadow counterpoint to credit. One complements and is completed by the other. Faith is based in this delicate balance. When I receive money in the form of credit, I undertake a covenant, a promise, to repay the amount provided. In good faith I will place as collateral the item I am acquiring with the money received, or something of equivalent value, to secure that debt. Although we may think of money as coins and currency, this represents a very small amount of the money in circulation. In today's world, money is the credit that fuels a multidimensional economic machine.

Banks create money when they extend credit. In our fractional reserve banking system, the debt created when a loan is made is used as a deposit on which to issue the credit. For example, let's say a bank deposits a reserve of one million dollars with the central bank, the Federal Reserve, and based upon that fractional reserve, may issue loans in the amount of nine million dollars. Credit is extended to borrowers who sign promissory notes—debt—that the bank shows as an asset on its balance sheet. Money is magically created out of nothing but a promise and a purpose. The promise is the debt collateralized by the purpose for which the borrower uses the credit. The borrower pledges the asset for which the money is spent, or other assets, as collateral for his ability to make good on the promise to repay the principal *and interest* of the loan. The borrower spends the money, and the seller deposits the money in another bank which also leverages that deposit to make additional loans on the ten to one fractional reserve basis. The advantage of this system is that credit can be rapidly brought to an economy on a highly leveraged basis. The downside is that there are not sufficient reserves backing the credit should the system contract and depositors demand repayment of their deposits.

The beginnings of the fractional reserve system go back to medieval Europe. Merchants concerned with protecting their money, primarily gold, placed the gold in the most secure place they could find, with the local goldsmith. The goldsmith determined he could make loans of these gold deposits in the form of notes backed by the underlying gold. Holders of these notes could demand, at any time, payment in gold. Over time the goldsmith discovered that only a small part of the total notes issued were required to meet this liquidity demand. Under normal conditions, he required only one-tenth of his total liability to be held in the physical asset and could earn huge profits on the credit he extended on this leveraged basis.

The danger came during periods of economic duress when depositors and creditors demanded at once payment in full of their deposits and the notes representing deposit. History is replete with stories of the many failures of the goldsmiths who foreshadowed the bankers of our modern system. It was this problem with liquidity in time of financial crisis that led to creating central banks whose purpose was to be a bank for the bankers during times when reserves were insufficient. The Bank of England was the first true central bank, and was the model for the banking system in this country.

As each bank makes additional loans, money is created in the form of the principal amount of credit. An interest rate is added on the principal. Over the course of the loan, especially long-term loans such as real estate mortgages, the amount of interest paid may greatly exceed the principal due on the debt. The money necessary to repay both the principal and the interest does not exist in the system because the only money created was for the amount of the principal. It is this scarcity of money to fund the interest payments that makes further money creation essential to provide liquidity in the system for interest payments. This also creates a competitive dynamic between borrowers to compete for scarce money resources.

The outcome of this system is that money flows to those who can best compete for the limited resources. Money migrates to a small percentage of the population. This creates economic and social distress. The lower rungs of the economic ladder have fewer resources available to purchase goods and services, with detrimental consequences to everyone. Economic duress leads to social malaise, often leading to political upheaval. This situation is well known to those who control the Money Power. Wealth transfer arrangements such as philanthropic activities, taxation, fiscal policy, and social welfare programs are in place to lessen the impact of the concentration of wealth.

Religious prohibitions against usury are well documented in Judaism, Christianity, and Islam. Usury is usually defined as unreasonable interest. A broader definition would include interest charged solely on money itself. The payment of interest was considered permissible in ancient times as long as the amount paid was earned from the productive outcome of the loan. A farmer could borrow grain for planting and repay, with interest, in grain obtained from the harvest. A loan in the form of a cow could be repaid in kind with a calf given as interest. Concern arose when the payment was obtained solely from the existence of money. Christ threw the moneychangers from the temple because their profit came entirely from the exploitation of money, with no productive activity engendering the process of the loan. In modern Islam, banks make loans as partners in the specific activity of the loan and receive interest from the profit of that effort. The payment of interest is then incorporated in an organic and integral way with productive wealth creation. "Jubilee Year" in ancient Israel was created to mitigate the disruptive effect of interest on society. As documented in Leviticus, every forty-nine years, Jubilee Year, all debts were forgiven.

These prohibitions against what is considered unreasonable interest are rooted in a deep sense of the moral nature of money and concern for the exploitation that naturally occurs from the effects of interest in a money system. Compound interest is a powerful force, but it does not exist in nature. It is a theoretical construct and unsustainable in any viable ecosystem. Although it may allow certain players to earn extreme profits for a short time, it becomes mathematically impossible for the process to continue indefinitely. Finite resources cannot sustain the open-ended outcomes of compounding.

The current national debt of the U.S. government is over nineteen trillion dollars, which is just over seventy-five thousand dollars per U.S. citizen. If the unfunded liabilities of Medicaid, Medicare, and Social Security are included, the amount balloons to sixty trillion, which increases the liability to over a half million dollars per family. Most families are already burdened with substantial personal debt, which renders infinitesimal the probability of this federal debt ever being repaid. By any accounting, the U.S. government faces a serious debt problem.

Money Power and the Moral Dilemma

> *"I care not what puppet is placed upon the throne of England to rule*
> *the empire on which the sun never sets. The man who controls Britain's money*
> *supply controls the British Empire, and I control the British money supply."*
> —Nathan Rothschild (1820)

The framers of the Constitution spent a great deal of time on governance and the separation of power. They, unfortunately, did not say much about money, and this oversight has resulted in a centuries-long clash of visions regarding money's role and purpose. Article I, Section 8 states that Congress shall have the power "To coin Money, regulate the value thereof..." and "To provide for the Punishment of counterfeiting the Securities and current Coin of the United States..." Article I, Section 10 gives Congress this power exclusively by stating that "No State shall... coin Money...."

At the time our nation was created, paper money was a relatively new concept. It had been used with some success in colonial times largely because England prohibited importing currency and the colonists had been forced to develop a money system. The fledgling Continental Congress financed the Revolutionary War primarily by issuing Continental currency. Although it financed a successful revolution, British counterfeiting greatly debased the currency. By the end of the war little confidence remained in fiat paper money.

A conflict between two competing visions of government's role regarding money marked the early days of our democracy. Federalists, led by Alexander Hamilton, believed in a privately owned central bank based upon the English model. Republicans, led by Jefferson and Madison, distrusted the private bankers and wanted the government to control money. Hamilton, with the support of powerful New York merchants, proposed and established a privately owned national bank, financed substantially by English and Dutch capital.

Jefferson opposed the First National Bank of the United States, and it lost its charter in 1811. The fledgling nation was ill equipped to be served by a hodgepodge of state banks, and the Second National Bank was chartered in 1817 for twenty years. Andrew Jackson and his successor, Martin Van Buren, distrusted the power vested in a strong central bank, and the story of their administrations focuses primarily on their battle with the bank. It was Van Buren who used the term "Money Power" when referring to those private bankers who controlled the nation's money supply.

Throughout the nineteenth century the battle waged between the proponents of a strong central bank and those who backed decentralized state banks. State banks were a nightmare of corruption and confusion. During the Civil War, Lincoln issued money directly from the government. These Greenbacks, though debased by inflation during the war, eventually were redeemed at par and became the cornerstone of the battle over money control at the end of the century.

On one side were the industrialists and financiers, known as the "robber barons" because lack of legal restraint at that time enabled them to accumulate huge fortunes through monopoly, exploitation, and outright theft. Rockefeller controlled the oil, and his banking arm was the Chase Manhattan Bank, financed largely with Rothschild backing. Morgan controlled finance and steel when he bought out Carnegie in 1901.

The Populists and the Greenback party, most famously represented by the great statesman and orator William Jennings Bryan, were in opposition and favored government-issued money. During the 1890s a groundswell arose against the Money Power. This was also a time of political upheaval throughout the world, and the voices of money reform were lost amid the cacophony of revolutionaries of every sort.

Wall Street bankers, through shrewd political and economic manipulation, were able to establish the Federal Reserve Bank in 1913. It is no coincidence that the federal income tax was also established that year with the passage of the Sixteenth Amendment. The sole purpose of the federal income tax, which the original framers of the Constitution never considered, was to finance the interest payments incurred through its debt to the Federal Reserve.

The Federal Reserve was established primarily in reaction to the bank liquidity crisis of the Panic of 1907. As the lender of last resort, the central bank is supposed to manage liquidity in the money supply. It has often proved less than capable in serving its primary purpose. This was demonstrated most dramatically during the total bank collapse of the Great Depression. Although reforms were put in place to regulate securities and monitor the separate functions of investment and commercial banking, these controls either have been rescinded, such as the repeal of the Glass Stiegel Act that had separated commercial and investment banking, or neglected, such as the outdated and irrelevant securities laws regulating financial markets. It is clear we have serious problems when the former chairman of the Federal Reserve, testifying before Congress in response to the recent bank collapse, confesses, "I have discovered a critical flaw in my ideology." Mr. Greenspan recognized what has long been apparent to many: greed trumps ideology.

The U.S. government does not create money, though this is what most Americans believe. The Federal Reserve Bank creates money. The Federal Reserve is neither federal nor based upon what most would consider realistic reserves. The Federal Reserve is comprised of twelve regional banks that commercial member banks own in proportion to their size. The New York Federal Reserve is considered first among equals, and its largest member banks are JP Morgan Chase and Citibank. Both banks trace their origin to the Rockefeller and Morgan financial empires. Although the President appoints the chairman of the Federal Reserve, who is approved by the Senate, private owners control the U. S. money supply. This puts the current government bailout in its true light. The Fed issues new capital to itself, the member owners who, through their corruption, greed, and mismanagement, bankrupted themselves. They create this money by putting the people of the United States into greater debt.

The Federal Reserve Notes we carry in our pockets are indeed printed by the Treasury, but for the Federal Reserve. Currency is a very small portion of the money supply, less than five percent. Most money is created in the form of debt. The U.S. government issues debt that it sells to the Federal Reserve who "monetizes" it. The member banks, which are required to maintain only a "fractional reserve" of the loans they make, multiply the money nine times over through creating commercial loans. Money is magically created out of thin air.

These are only the loans banks show on their financial statements. The explosion of unregulated derivative securities has become a lucrative source of additional revenue for these bankers who are not content with earning interest on money they have created with nothing more than an entry in an accounting ledger. These outside bets exist off balance sheet. Though this sort of accounting chicanery would land most of us in prison, the bankers receive an exemption from the Money Power. In spite of this advantage, their greed has driven them to extinction as they have pursued obscene profits through leverage and outright fraud.

While the bankers reap the windfall, the American people are stuck with the principal and interest payments for this national debt. As we have demonstrated, repayment is mathematically impossible. This is the crux of the moral dilemma. As a sovereign nation governed by the rule of law and dedicated to a government of the people, by the people, and for the people, should we citizens abdicate the authority to create and maintain our money power and cede that control to a private banking cartel?

The moral question goes to the heart of money. Who controls money and for what purpose? Does money exist solely for the benefit of those best able to exploit it for reasons of self-interest? Or is money a common utility to be shared for the common good? These questions have been posed when society has had to determine the proper control and utilization of common resources such as water, air, and energy. Water is considered a right of the people, and control for private use is strictly regulated. We recognize that, although the electric grid may be privately owned, electricity pricing and distribution are controlled for the public welfare. Yet regarding money, possibly the most important of all natural resources in terms of public utility and the advancement of our prime directive as a nation dedicated to life, liberty, and the pursuit of happiness, a small but powerful private financial cartel holds control.

Money is a theoretical concept. It exists not as an absolute reality unto itself but as a tool to enable and support human beings on their evolutionary journey. Aristotle called it *nomisma*. In *Nicomachean Ethics*[11] he says, "Money exists not by nature but by law *(nomos)*."

Money has often been thought of as a commodity, a naturally existing entity, because every monetary system has been challenged to provide a standard of measurement and value for the underlying theoretical legal entity. Yet the two are distinct to their nature and to their design. Money exists by law. Law is a set of moral and ethical structures and rules designed to support and protect society.

We institute systems of governance and control to regulate and maintain our moral and legal precepts in order to support and sustain our law. In the same manner, money standards are implemented to support and maintain money. Commodities, primarily precious metals, have served that purpose in the past. Yet the systems of old must evolve with humanity. The scroll gave way to the printed page, which has been humbled by the digital screen. Communication exists in all. The need for money standards should not blind us from the true nature of money and who must have control of its massive power.

This conflict between money as law and money as commodity has clouded the history of money. The founders of our nation were schooled in Adam Smith who thought of money solely as a commodity. Issues of standards of measurement and proper reserve requirements have led us to lose sight of the true nature and basic essence of money. Money is credit. Credit is founded in trust. Trust is a moral virtue. Any viable money must be based upon this foundation. Aspects of measurement and control, though important, are not the primary determinant of money.

Every ecosystem struggles to grow and prosper against often unknown obstacles. They must be efficient in accomplishing their productive goals and resilient in maintaining protection against detrimental effects. The two aspects are often at odds. In maximizing efficient production, the system may become unable to maintain sufficient resiliency to external causation. In contrast, a system overly concerned with protective resiliency may become unresponsive to its primary goals. A successful ecosystem, whether a human body, a corporate entity, or a national and world economy, must find the precise balance point that allows prolonged sustainability with equal parts efficiency and resiliency. Our current monetary system, indeed our entire corporate consumer economy in its single-minded focus on maximizing efficiency in the pursuit of greater productivity and higher profit, has overshot resiliency. The natural result of this will be continued stress of the entire system.

The Evil Empire

I grew up a child of the fifties and sixties and learned the evils of communism at an early age. Over time I've come to grips with many interior demons, not the least my conditioning regarding the communist boogieman. The first step was my recognizing that Karl Marx and Fredric Engels did not conceive and write their philosophies in the bowels of hell at the behest of Satan.

Conversely, the concept of capitalism, based upon the market theories of Ricardo, Smith, and others and rooted in the enlightenment philosophies of Locke and others was not commissioned by the Lord God almighty, regardless of what some current politicians and religious leaders may fervently believe. If anything, the basic precept of communism, from each according to his ability to each according to his need, sounds Christian. Many passages in the gospels would support Jesus Christ as the author of the original communist manifesto, although one in particular exemplifies the overriding concern Jesus had for the poor and the downtrodden. In one parable, a rich young man asked Jesus what good deeds he must do to earn eternal life. Jesus first listed the usual Jewish litany of keeping the commandments. The man replied, "All these I have observed; what do I still lack?" Jesus said to him, "If you would be perfect go, sell what you posses and give to the poor, and you will have treasure in heaven; and come follow me." When the young man heard this, he went away sorrowful, for he had great possessions. (*The Bible*, Matthew 19:16-30, Mark 10:17-31, Luke 18:18-30) The young man's sorrow is understandable. It is difficult to meet such a high standard of detachment.

Communism as a social theory is soundly rooted in moral values and a rigorous methodology based upon Hegelian philosophy. Its premise is that the social welfare of society's majority class should not be subjugated to the economic interests of a ruling minority. Unfortunately, though it may be good social theory as an economic system, communism flounders primarily because it does not acknowledge the basic human nature that it purports to champion. Individuals are more motivated by the prospect of personal gratification than they are by the dream of a collective utopia. Whereas they may acknowledge the dream, they have little motivation to take the initiative to achieve group goals. A "let the other guy do it" mentality takes hold, lowering productivity. Also the evil aspect of communism is directly linked to the unfortunate historical development that found the first prototype of communist ideology adopted in Russia, an absolute monarchy still rooted in a feudal economic system. Marx had always envisioned the rise of the proletariat within the structure of western society that had established the tensions so necessary for his class struggle. The evils of Soviet communism are much more rooted in a sociopolitical tradition going back to Ivan the Terrible than in a somewhat misguided socioeconomic theory.

Communism may have some social merit providing psychotic despots don't implement it, but as an economic model it has a poor track record. The Soviet Union was a terrible testing ground for the value of communist economic theory. It was difficult to encourage production while murdering thirty million of the work force, as was the case with Joseph Stalin. Western countries that adopted some of the precepts of communism made the medicine a bit more palatable by calling it socialism, but the basic premise is the same: the means of production is owned collectively rather than privately. However, many of these socialist countries enjoy affordable education and national health care.

First Effect of Credit: Competition

Where communism and its more attractive cousin, socialism, may be credited with some social props, when it comes to competing for scarce investment capital on a world stage, neither system had a chance against capitalist competitors. In an open market, pitting capitalism against communism is comparable to putting a pit bull in the ring with a miniature poodle. Although communism aspires to high social achievements, its economic record is abysmal. In contrast, capitalism is a theory somewhat soft on social welfare but exceedingly efficient as an economic system. The past century demonstrated that the benefits of free, open market economies provide the best opportunity for increasing the standard of living for most citizens of countries in a position to implement such a system. Capitalism's biggest problem is that it works too well.

Same Church, Different Pew

It is important to differentiate the economic and political theories of the two competing economic theories of the twentieth century from the supporting monetary system. The underlying money base for the entire world has been a credit-based system of national currency. The Soviet Union did not create its own monetary system distinct and separate from the rest of the world. Although it was possible to enslave citizens and ignore reality and the rest of the world—does North Korea come to mind?—the fact is that the world's money base exists for all nations, regardless of their beliefs, confusions, or outright delusions. Communism failed as a political-economic system because it could not compete with capitalism in the world credit markets.

The fundamental reason for this is explicit in the credit-based monetary system. Let's review how money is created in a credit system:

1. Saver one has deposited $100 in bank one. Each now has $100.

2. Bank one lends $90 to borrower one, keeping $10 in reserve.

3. Borrower one deposits the $90 in bank two, which lends out $80 to borrower two. The original $100 has now magically become $270 as the banks created money through loans on credit. It's a good system as long as there is sufficient trust in the system and liquidity to avoid a run on assets, which we can see do not meet the liabilities. Now let's take it a little further:

4. Although $270 of new money has been created at each level of credit, the issuing bank will require the payment of interest on the loan.

5. If each bank required the annual payment of five percent interest on the loan each year, borrower one must pay $4.50 to bank one, and borrower two must pay $4.00 to bank two. This money was not created in the initial credit process, however. The only source is from the original loans, and each borrower is competing with the other to obtain their required interest payment from the other borrower's principal.

Though this example is simplistic and assumes a closed system with no growth or increase in productivity, it does represent the basic nature of competition in our credit-based monetary system. This does not mean the system is bad. To the contrary, the competitive nature focuses participants' efforts on productivity and, as we have seen over the last three hundred years, increases in economic productivity have rewarded the winners, western countries, with unprecedented levels of economic prosperity.

Often our greatest strength may be out greatest weakness. Let's use another simple example. Remember as a kid on the playground when it was time to pick teams? Usually the two best athletes were designated captains and flipped a coin or otherwise determined who would have first pick. The winner chose the person she thought best qualified to achieve victory, and the draft continued down to the invariably humiliating end of seeing who was chosen last. Now imagine that after the competition the victor got to trade their worst player for the losing team's best player. Assuming the teams continue to play to their best ability, it is easy to see that soon one team would have all the best players. This is the Achilles heel of free market capitalism. Those adept at competing within the system get richer and those who are less adept get poorer. J. Paul Getty, once the richest man in the world, was asked why he did not give away all his money. "In five years," he replied, "I would have it all back, and more." He certainly understood the competitive nature of our credit-based monetary system.

Second Effect of Credit: Concentration of Wealth

In addition to competition, our monetary system requires endless growth and concentrates wealth. In our example of how interest works, we assumed zero population, production, or money supply growth. The force of compound interest is staggering. Historically, societies attempted to "lay away" some money as a means to meet the inexorable growth of interest and the weight it brings on an economic system.

In the _Bible_, the story of the Joseph penny provides a graphic description of the immensity of the influence of compound interest over time. If at the birth of Jesus, Joseph had invested one penny earning interest at four percent per year, by the year 1749 the value of that account would have equaled the value of a ball of gold the weight of the earth. By 1990 that value would have increased to the weight in gold of 8,190 balls the size of the earth.

The ancient prophets of Israel must have had some economic training. They recognized the potential destructive power of compound interest and stated their prohibition of usury in no uncertain terms. "He that hath given in usury and hath taken increase shall he live? He shall not live: he hath done all these abominations; he shall surely die, his blood shall be upon him." (the _Bible_, Ezekiel 18:13) In ancient times a debt moratorium every seven years forgave all accrued debts, action that provided balance to a system that could not sustain its ever mounting debt. (the _Bible_, Deuteronomy 15)

Third Effect of Credit: Transfer of Wealth

Our credit-based system tends to transfer wealth from the majority to a small minority of people. In a German study in 1982 the entire population was divided into groups based on household income. During the year a total of DM270 billion in interest payments passed among all of the groups. The net effect was a transfer of DM34.2 billion from the bottom nine groups to the top ten percent. In the United States, the top one percent of the population owns as much personal wealth as the bottom ninety-two percent of the country. The three richest people in the world have more wealth than the poorest forty-eight nations combined. Since this study wealth has continued to concentrate in the top fraction of one percent of the U.S. population especially following the financial crisis of 2008–2009.

Much like cream rises to the top of milk, so, too, does wealth move inexorably to the top economic tier in a credit-based monetary system. It is a necessary by-product. The efficiencies that are the blessing of the system become the curse. It is easy to recognize that, over time, the concentration of wealth within too narrow an economic class will precipitate both social and economic malaise. Socially, the "have-nots" will attempt to take what they cannot win through their efforts within the system by establishing a new system or violently subjugating the old one. Economically, as the bottom levels of the economic base become less wealthy the system will have a shrinking base upon which to grow. Eventually, business shrinks and the whole top-heavy structure crumbles under its own weight.

This is why a capitalist, free-market economy with a credit-based monetary system always needs to develop mechanisms for the transfer of wealth from the top down. The means run from taxation and other government fiscal policies to outright wealth transfer programs. Whereas the top ten percent of the wealthy generally object to such actions as either unfair or outright criminal, they need to understand that without some form of transfer in place, the system cannot continue. We've all heard tales of the greed and ruthless competitive spirit of industrial giants who amassed great fortunes throughout history. Less recognized, however, is that many of these successful entrepreneurs understood the need to "pay back." Our country's philanthropic organizations, such as the Carnegie, Ford, MacArthur, and Bill and Melinda Gates Foundations, serve as effective conduits of wealth transfer done under the conscious guidance of the donors. Warren Buffet has provided the means for his entire fortune to be given to philanthropy and has created an organization of like-minded billionaires encouraging them to do the same.

In addition to government policies, which by definition will be imperfect, and the much more efficient contributions made from individual contributions, we can help our economic and monetary system find the balance it so desperately needs for its continued existence. Complementary currencies offer the promise for a more balanced approach to money.

Each of the three effects of credit has positive and negative aspects relative to the economy and to society. Competition can be a positive motivating force that creates an environment for focused productivity. When we perform to the best of our ability and achieve the fruits of our efforts through victory, whether on the sporting field or in the marketplace, we experience a feeling of achievement and satisfaction. Many of humanity's great triumphs in the fields of art, science, and technology are the result of the competitive spirit found in humans. Yet that positive competitive spirit has its time and place.

There is a time for winners (and the necessary losers) and there is a time for cooperation with no view to individual victory, but rather a total focus on the needs and efforts of the entire group. Think of a crisis situation, the bombing of the World Trade Center, for example. The tales of heroism and sacrifice of the office workers and the police and firefighters who gave their lives in rescue attempts do not include tales of competition. Anyone who ever faced enemy fire in combat will tell you that the survival of each soldier depends on the concerted cooperative actions of the entire unit, from the commander on down. Individual acts of extreme bravery are almost always inspired by the needs of the entire unit, rather than some competitive desire for individual glory. No one should ever have to experience war or terrorism, but it's a fact that fame-seeking glory hunters do not last long on the battlefield.

Everyone experiences the need for balance between healthy competition and conscious cooperation. Health care is a good example. The concerted efforts to eradicate famine, advance drug and medical technology, and ensure that clean water and sanitary conditions are rights enjoyed by all have increased life expectancy. Competition has increased drug development to combat diseases once considered incurable. Yet where competition enhances development, it can also hinder implementation. In spite of a dramatic reduction in uninsured Americans following the implementation of The Affordable Care Act (Obamacare) over twenty million Americans continue to not have health insurance. Costs continue to rise dramatically, yet insurance companies spend billions of private health on commercial advertising directed not at the physician prescribing the drugs but at the consumer. While these companies are provided the freedom to advertise Medicare is prohibited from taking advantage of purchasing power to negotiate lower drug costs, presumably because the politicians supporting this clear infringement on free market capitalism value their campaign contributions from Big Pharma more than they do the welfare of Medicare recipients.

Ideally, insurance companies are in the business of paying claims, not collecting premiums. The greatest medicines and medical technology are worthless if a society cannot determine a way to implement health care in a comprehensive, cooperative manner. This is one area where large numbers are essential to manage the risk of a common liability, in this case the need for quality, affordable health care for all members of a society. If competition and cooperation cannot be balanced in pursuit of a shared need then the system is failing.

The drive toward competition is partly hardwired in our primitive brain, a by-product of our early development when survival depended on any slight competitive edge, and is partly derived from environmental and social factors. The basic polarization differences between men and women also determine the competitive drive. As we will discuss in Chapter Six, men are primarily electric in their polarization while women are primarily magnetic. In a *New York Times* op ed piece,[12] of May 25, 2005, John Tierney reported the different attitudes towards competition between men and women.

He told how economists recently tried to determine this in an experiment in Pittsburgh by paying men and women to add up five numbers in their heads. At first they worked individually, doing as many sums as they could in five minutes and receiving 50 cents for each correct answer. Then they competed in four-person tournaments, with the winner getting two dollars per correct answer and the losers getting nothing. On average, the women made as much as the men under either system. But when they were offered a choice for the next round—take the piece rate or compete in a tournament—most women declined to compete, even the ones who had done the best in the earlier rounds. Most men chose the tournament, even the ones who had done the worst. The men's eagerness partly stemmed from overconfidence, because on average men rated their ability more highly than the women rated theirs. But interviews and further experiments convinced the researchers,

Muriel Niederle of Stanford and Lise Vesterlund of the University of Pittsburgh, that the gender gap wasn't due mainly to women's insecurities about their abilities. It was due to different appetites for competition.

"Even in tasks where they do well, women seem to shy away from competition, whereas men seem to enjoy it too much," Professor Niederle said. "The men who weren't good at this task lost a little money by choosing to compete, and the good women passed up a lot of money by not entering tournaments they would have won."

You can argue that this difference is due to social influences, although I suspect it's largely innate, a by-product of evolution and testosterone. Whatever the cause, it helps explain why men set up the traditional corporate ladder as one continual winner-take-all competition—and why that structure no longer makes sense.

As we discussed earlier in this chapter, there are behavioral archetypes that are embedded deep within the collective subconscious of the human psyche. Each archetype may manifest in different aspects. When one aspect of the archetype is repressed in the human psyche, rather than integrated into consciousness in a balanced manner, it will manifest in behavior that is not healthy for either the individual or society as a whole. In *Of Human Wealth*,[10] Bernard Lietaer and Stephen Belgin explain these different fundamental aspects as they relate to money from a Taoist perspective identified in the balance of energies of Yin (feminine/magnetic) and Yang (masculine/electric). Some traits characterizing the Yin and Yang aspects of money are:

Yang	Yin
Competition	Cooperation
Having	Being
Peak experience	Endurance-sustainability
Logic, linear	Paradoxical, non-linear
Technology	Interpersonal skills
Bigger is better	Small is beautiful
Hierarchy works best	Egalitarian works best
Central authority	Mutual trust
Transcendent God	Immanent Divinity

These traits are not independent or mutually exclusive. They are the polar aspects of a unified whole. For there to be harmony, the traits need to be in balance. There is a time for competition and a time for cooperation, a time for logic and a time for paradox, and a time to recognize the infinite transcendence of God and the immanent divinity in all creation. Problems arise when these diverse traits are not balanced and either Yin or Yang aspects are dominant. Our current monetary system is dominated by Yang energies. A positive money future depends on integrating Yin energies into the system.

In the same sense, growth can be positive and essential to any healthy organism whether an individual or a collective construct of society. Just as uncontrolled growth in a living organism will lead to the destruction of that organism, so, too, will the need for constant growth put pressures on an economic system that will do anything to maintain the required growth, even if the actions taken are not in the long-term interest of the overall system. In any healthy organic system—human, government, or corporation—there is a time for birth, growth, stasis, decline, and a time to end. There is grace, elegance, and beauty when we recognize life's natural flow and merge within it. In contrast, when we ignore the facts of life in misguided, self-absorbed illusions founded solely on theoretical constructs, greedy self-interest, and outright pathological behavior, the results can be both catastrophic and tragic.

Complementary Currencies

In many ways the history of money is the story of different forms of money or currency serving in a complementary manner, depending on the need of those using the currency or the function of the particular currency. It is only with the dominance of national currencies, the dollar in particular, that we have come to view complementary currencies as something foreign or exotic.

If complementary currencies share one key element, it is that they are based upon some form of barter or exchange. In Japan, for example, the challenges of caring for an aging population are supported with a complementary healthcare currency that allows volunteers to accumulate time that can be credited to their accounts. They can then redeem these credits for their elder relatives' care anywhere in the country. Community currencies such as this can greatly assist the use of excess capacity, especially during times when conventional currency may be in short supply.

The Terra

On an international level, the proposed creation of an international complementary currency, the terra is especially intriguing. Currently the greatest risk for any business engaged in international commerce is not market or political risk, but currency risk. The level of currency speculation and the volatility associated with floating rates of exchange can wipe out all profit from any business activity in a short time. In an attempt to manage this risk, many international transactions are bartered. It is estimated that over fifteen percent of all international commerce operates on some sort of barter system. For example, Pepsi, at one time, received much of the payment for its product sold in Russia not in rubles, but in vodka. Yet the old problems of barter remain. It is not easy to transport tons of vodka, and not everyone will value the product in the same manner.

The terra would be an international currency based upon the value of a market basket of international commodities such as a barrel of oil, ounce of silver, bushel of corn, etc. An oil producer, for example, would deposit excess oil capacity with the currency-issuing holding company and receive a corresponding value of terras. The producer could use the terras to pay service providers who would use them to meet their expenses. As the terras worked through the system, at some point a holder would redeem them for their corresponding national currency. This would provide a stabilizing factor for currency speculation and the effect of inflation, as well as help smooth inventory and cash-flow issues during market recessions.

In addition, whereas credit currencies reward the creditor with interest payments, complementary currencies often have a demurrage charge. This resembles reverse interest because it is a charge placed upon the holder of a currency over time. For instance, if I hold a currency valued at one hundred dollars for one year with a three-percent annual demurrage fee, then I will be charged three dollars. This feature discourages hoarding currency and makes it an excellent medium of short-term exchange. The terra would have such a feature, which would pay for the cost of stockpiling the commodities underlying the value of the currency.

Bitcoin is a digital currency first introduced in 2009. It bypasses all national banks and currencies and is based upon digital transactions between bitcoin wallets operating on a network that runs on a protocol known as a blockchain, which is designed to guarantee the authenticity of the transaction. Initially the bitcoin was used as a means to avoid government scrutiny for the funding of illegal operations but more recently has gained popularity for both investment and business purpose.

Credit currencies are essential to the continued economic function of the planet. The addition of complementary currencies is not an alternative, but rather a true complement to support and enhance the existing world and national monetary systems. Complementary systems should not be viewed as attempts to supplant the existing system. They are additions better suited for addressing specific needs the current system does not meet. Rather than fear complementary currencies as a threat to our current banking system, we should embrace the prospect of what they have to offer with open arms, recognizing they can balance and enhance the world of money. Alternately, if we ignore complementary currencies and the energy they engender, we are likely to see our present monetary system continue to grow and develop, but with ever increasing imbalances and ever more frequent financial crises, with the attending unavoidable misery and suffering a system undergoes when pushed to the breaking point.

Future Money

It is good to look to the past to understand the future of money. We have seen how money's origins are related to the earliest human actions: the need to survive, to obtain shelter and food, and propagate the species. Money is, at heart, nourishment—physical, emotional, and spiritual. This history of money is represented vividly on the five-dollar bill, with Abraham Lincoln on one side framed in sprays of wheat and the magnificent Lincoln monument, built in the style of an ancient Greek temple with thirty-six Doric columns representing the thirty-six states of the Union, on the other. It is Lincoln who represents, more than any other president, the sense of unity and the melding of the ideals and values at the foundation of our nation.

We have seen how the word money came from Monetta, a name of the goddess Juno, whose temple served as the earliest mint. Monetta was also the name of the goddess Aequitas, who signified equity, or fair allotment, provided by the state to its citizens. Money is essential in the organization of community. If this is true, then perhaps the best definition we can provide for money is "money is a symbol of grace."

Without community and a sense of meaning found in relationships within a vibrant community, life loses its meaning and vitality. In a good community, the members love and respect each other not out of a sense of duty or obligation, but out of recognition of the inner abundance of spirit that is the basis for the community. A divine cosmic transcendence, yet manifest in the daily lives of the community, lies at the heart of this moral order. Money, so closely identified with the shared family meal and the survival of the community, is a symbol for this divine order working in our lives. When we become obsessed solely with the material aspects of money and allow it to appeal only to our lower emotions such as fear and greed, money falls short of its potential. William Desmonde[13] said it well in his book, *Magic, Myth and Money*:

> "It is only by actualizing the higher potentialities symbolized by money that justice can be secured within large organizations and emotional fulfillment restored to our producing and consuming activities. To do so we must attain the insight and the courage to think of money in its true sense, as a symbol of grace. Man's deepest happiness stems from his identification with the creative energies of nature, whereby the individual dedicates himself to the advancement of civilization. Grace may therefore be construed as the awakening within a person of this insight into his real nature. Grace is divine inspiration."

Thus money has evolved from the satisfaction of the physical needs of the individual, family, and tribal unit to a representation of the divine within the fabric of society. Grace can be defined as elegance and beauty of form, manner, or action. It can denote special favor or mercy. In the context of money, I think the appropriate definition is the one Desmonde has chosen: the freely given, unmerited favor and love of God, the influence or spirit of God operating in man. It is from and through money that the divine manifests and works in the world and it is our grace as human beings with souls through which we can realize our true divine nature. Money is grace. Grace is consciousness. Our life's work is to realize our highest purpose. If we are to succeed, we must be fully conscious. We must awaken our MoneyForce and find balance in our relationship with and to money.

3
Being and Sustainability

"One must be something, in order to do something."
—Johann Wolfgang von Goethe

"If we cannot have what we like, we must learn to like what we have."
—John Paul Jones

The future of money depends in large part on the choices people will make during the next decade. If we continue to choose having over being and model economic prosperity on eighteenth century economic and social models, then we face a future of great extremes. Wealth will continue to concentrate in the hands of the top one percent of the population and the division of rich and poor will widen. As we deplete our precious natural resources to enable developing nations to live at U.S. and European standards, we will see increased strain on the carrying capacity of our planet.

On the other hand, if we choose being as our first choice and allot it to its natural priority in our age-old pursuit of wealth and happiness, we can establish a bright future for money and the well-being of most of the earth's inhabitants. It is not a question of either/or, but a question of priority and balance, with the central focus placed on being and living within an economic structure of sustainability. Although this shift is occurring on a grassroots level—as millions of people are demonstrating through ever increasing consciousness and awareness— a repressive backlash and radical religious intolerance and fanaticism exist concurrently. Local communities must organize to create the foundations for a culture of being and sustainability. It is only from this position that national leaders will emerge to take our planet to a new golden era of awareness, peace, and prosperity.

Sarah James and Torbjorn Lahti present a model for communities to move toward sustainability in their book, *The Natural Step for Communities*.[14] They begin with the premise that there are natural system condition steps:

In the sustainable society, nature is not subject to systematically increasing:

1. Concentrations of substances extracted from the earth's crust
2. Concentrations of substances produced by society
3. Degradation by physical means

And, in that society,

4. Human needs are met worldwide

From these conditions they then set four sustainability objectives:

1. Reduce wasteful dependence upon fossil fuels, scarce metals, and minerals that accumulate in nature
2. Reduce wasteful dependence upon chemicals and synthetic substances that accumulate in nature
3. Reduce encroachment upon nature
4. Meet human needs fairly and efficiently

These goals may appear theoretical and unrealistic but they are, in fact, being put into practice in towns and villages, not only in Sweden, but throughout the world. As these pioneering communities demonstrate the feasibility and benefit of sustainable economies, others will recognize that these steps are not a dream but a reality.

Our Choice

Change is seldom easy. There are always easy answers to easy questions, but if we are asking difficult questions that challenge us at the depths of our innermost, heartfelt desires, then the answers and the process for following the path that those answers prescribe will be challenging. The greatest feeling of fulfillment and success comes after we give our best and work as fully as we are able to achieve the goals we have set for ourselves.

The first choice begins with you. Ask yourself: "Will I accept the responsibility and opportunity to take the steps required to activate my MoneyForce, come into balance, and begin to recognize and realize my true birthright?" If you answered yes, you are ready to begin the journey.

4
Money in Time

"Andromeda, our closest sizable neighbor, is 2,200,000 light years away, and beyond it space falls away abysmally, nebula after nebula, island universe after island universe, until we reach the limits of our known universe some 26 billion light-years 'across' whatever that means in a four-dimensional pseudosphere."
—Huston Smith[15]

This book is not about money. It is about achieving true wealth and happiness and recognizing the inner nature of money. Money is inextricably linked with our lives. It can be a cruel dictator holding us hostage to our own limited lower natures as we continue to repeat a cycle of greed and fear with no true happiness and fulfillment.

We have the free will, however, to choose money as grace, the grace that will provide us the means to fulfill our heart's innermost desires and goals. If you choose to make money another grace in your ever increasingly grace-filled life, we hope the stories we share, the lessons we provide, and the exercises we suggest will inspire you to take the steps necessary for you to find your MoneyForce and make it a guiding light.

In Chapter One we looked at the role money played throughout history and how it developed over time. In this chapter we will explore money's place in time. History is not time. It takes place within the physical plane and is bound by the laws and restraints of time and space. It is a remembrance, a reflection of one possible reality. Truth comes in many forms. There is truth, relative truth, and absolute truth. History deals in the realm of truth and relative truth. Time is the arbiter of absolute truth.

For much of our history on this planet, humans existed in small bands of hunter-gatherers eking out a subsistence living. Recorded history takes us with some degree of confidence to about 3,000 B.C., and archeology has discovered evidence of advanced human social activity during the Agricultural Revolution up to about 10,000 B.C. What took place in between the advent of more developed social hierarchies and the first written records? There are many gaps in history that must be filled in through other means.

Where history ends, magic, myth, and dreams begin. We have no historical evidence of a Garden of Eden with Adam and Eve as the two original humans, yet millions of Christians, Jews and Muslims hold this belief at the core of their religious being. What is the difference between magic, myth, and dreams? Dreams can be real, overwhelming, and provide intense inspiration, comfort, and guidance, yet do not exist in history as we know it. As far as history is concerned, one third of everyone's life is spent dormant in bed, unrecorded and passive. Magic, as we discussed earlier, is an illusion. We know it is not real in a historic sense, but that realization does not alter our perception that what we are seeing is indeed happening. Illusion and reality are easily mistaken and truth exists in degrees.

Time is measured in the large and the small, and somewhere in the seemingly boundless reaches of uncountable universes time folds back upon itself. In abstract terms, time is a concept measured in relative space. If we think of existence as a set of nested planes of consciousness, each one independent but integrated with the others, it would look like The Great Nest of Being diagram that follows. Each plane exists on a low and high level, with the low manifesting lower levels of consciousness and the corresponding, less desirable conditions that are often expressed through negative energy. The higher levels radiate the purer, positive manifestations of that particular consciousness plane. Thus on the low physical, we find conditions of basic survival and instinct, often manifested in violent forms. On the high physical, we find expressions of physical fulfillment and fecundity.

Specific colors corresponding to each level emanate the energy of that level. These color energies originate at the highest monadic levels and come from the unmanifest to the manifest. The physical elements of air, water, earth, and fire, as well as ether, are associated with a specific plane of consciousness. Earth element is associated with the physical plane and the color brown or red. The color pale blue and water element are linked to the astral plane while pale yellow and air element influence the mental plane. Ether and fire element are associated with the soul plane with the color of pale violet. In general pale colors carry magnetic energy and will provide for more receptivity than will bright vivid colors that are electric. There are at least twelve evolutionary consciousness planes ranging from the densest (first) to the highest (twelfth). The path of evolution presents the downward movement during the involutionary from higher to denser planes of consciousness. Our evolutionary growth takes us from the denser planes to higher more subtle levels of understanding and consciousness.

This model of body to feelings to mind to spirit is at the foundation of the world's religions and the basis for much of the higher spiritual teachings common to all religious beliefs. It is what Huston Smith calls The Great Chain of Being or The Great Nest of Being because each succeeding level of consciousness includes but transcends the preceding level.

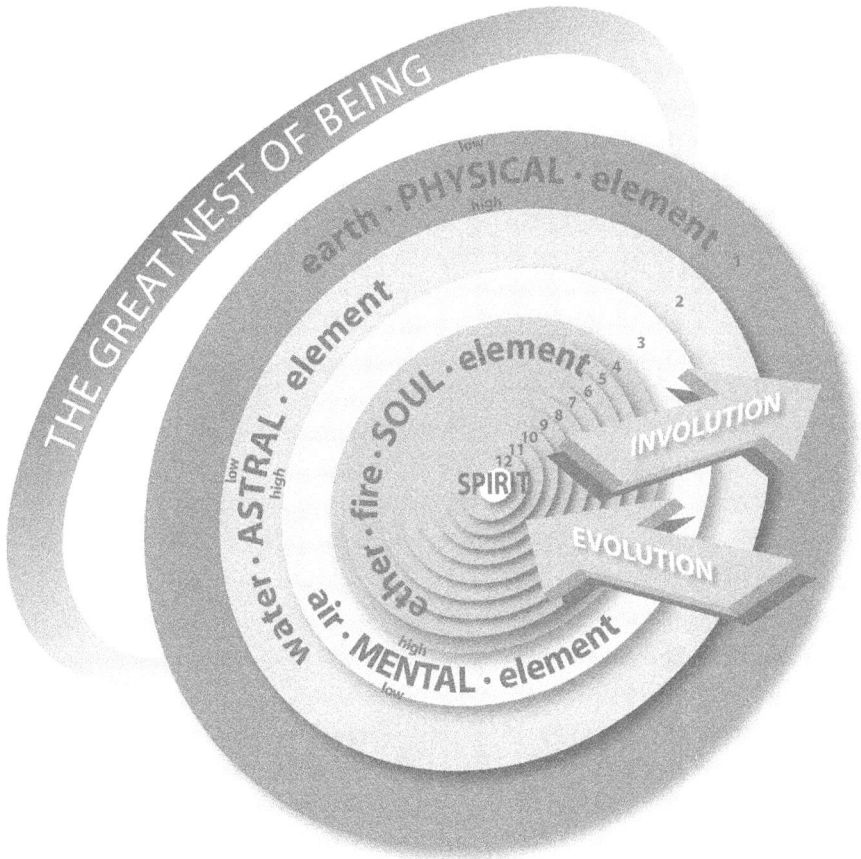

The Great Nest of Being

Before we begin to explore how our understanding and relationship to and with money is directly integrated with this model, it will help our discussion to review important work Ken Wilber has done. Wilber's unique contribution to philosophy and human consciousness is his astounding ability to integrate just about every school of thought on a myriad of topics into a cohesive working whole. He believes truth is in every system, at some level. Rather than reject every opposing belief based upon the differences held by each, we should focus on areas where opposing beliefs can agree. Out of these patterns that connect, or as he calls them "orienting generalizations," he has been able to develop an integrated "theory of everything." These patterns that connect are expressed in twenty tenets. Following is an explanation of the first five tenets:

Tenet number 1

Arthur Koestler coined the term "holon." Reality is composed of hole-parts, or holons. Everything is in everything. An atom is a whole part of a molecule which is a hole part of a cell which a whole part of a larger organism which is a whole part of an eco system which is a whole part of a biosphere which is a whole part of...you get the idea.

Tenet number 2

All holons share common traits in that every holon must always maintain its wholeness (agency) and its being a part of something else (communion). If a holon fails to maintain both, it cannot exist.

Tenet number 3

Holons unfold or emerge through process or evolution. There is direction in the Cosmos.

Tenet number 4

Holons emerge holarchically. Holarchy is Koestler's term for natural hierarchy. A natural hierarchy is simply an order of increasing wholeness such as particles to atoms to cells to organisms, or letters to words to sentences to paragraphs. The whole of one level becomes a part of the whole of the next.

Tenet number 5

Each emergent holon transcends but includes its predecessor(s). For example, the cell transcends—or goes beyond—its molecular components, but also includes them. Molecules transcend and include atoms, which transcend and include particles. The point is that because all holons are whole/parts, the wholeness transcends but the parts are included.

With these basic tenets as a foundation, Wilber presents ideas first introduced by professor of psychology Clare W. Graves and more fully developed by Don Edward Beck and Christoper C. Cowen in their book *Spiral Dynamics*.[16] Graves believed that mankind was on a heroic quest for meaning and purpose. At each level of this quest, we can identify stages associated with the particular aspects of the quest that is manifest at that time of development. As certain needs and questions are answered at each stage of development, man evolves to ever higher and more developed expressions of the never-ending quest.

The central premise of Graves and Cowen and Beck is that in any organization, levels of psychological existence and belief structures provide the organizing principle or the way people think and adjust to changing conditions. They call these levels MEMEs. Eight core MEMEs form a spiral and are represented by different colors. MEME sounds a lot like gene. Genes are the informational units of our molecular DNA and determine much of our biophysical nature. So, too, are MEMEs the basic structures of our psycho-cultural makeup. Beck and Cowen focused their application to the workplace to enable business leaders to understand and manage employees better, whereas Wilber integrated the concept of spiraling MEMEs in the context of an evolving cosmos.

MEMEs

In any organizational structure, whether a corporation, a nation, or the entire world population, people associate with a particular MEME. This will determine how they act and relate to their existence.

Beige: Structured in loose bands and underpinned by survival processes.

Beige thinking is automatic, and we use instinct and habits just to stay alive. Hunter-gathers are preoccupied with obtaining the basic needs of survival and are in the beige MEME.

Purple: Structured in tribe-like groups and underpinned by circular processes. Purple thinking is animistic and magical with a focus on keeping the spirits happy and supportive of the tribe. As tribal culture develops, magic and myth dominate the purple worldview with much of life preoccupied with animism.

Red: Structured by empires and underpinned by exploitive, power-seeking processes. Red thinking is egocentric. There are no constraints to individual desire. In a world of predators, the strongest will conquer and rule. With the development of city states and centralized authority, we enter the red MEME of warrior kings and absolute authority.

Blue: Pyramidal form and underpinned by purposeful, controlling, or even authoritarian processes. For the blue thinker, life has meaning and direction and there are absolute predetermined outcomes. Laws, righteous living, and highly structured social organizations ensure stability. In the blue MEME, obedience to law and authority is central.

Orange: Structured in delegative forms, underpinned by strategic, achievement-oriented, and autonomy-seeking processes. Orange thinking is open to multiple inputs, and change and advancement are welcomed. The orange MEME is much less hierarchical and fosters individual achievement.

Green: Structured in an egalitarian fashion, underpinned by processes that are both experiential and consensual. Green thinking is relativistic with a focus on inner growth, peace with others, the development of caring communities, and the desire for absolute equality. The green MEME loves the collective and wants to include everyone.

Yellow: Flexible, integrative, and knowledge-based both as a structure and in its processes. The yellow thinker believes there is a natural hierarchy of forms and systems and our purpose is to live fully with focus on what we are and who we can become. The yellow MEME understands there are natural hierarchies that must be acknowledged.

Turquoise: Holistic and global in structure, flowing and multidimensional in its processes. Turquoise thinking is holistic, and the goal is to experience the whole of existence through mind and spirit. The turquoise MEME embraces a holistic integration of body, mind, feelings, and spirit

Each succeeding MEME includes and transcends the previous MEME. It is necessary for the development of the organization for each MEME to be a healthy expression and not manifest repressed negative traits in the succeeding MEME. For example, when the red MEME manifests in a negative fashion in the blue MEME, we get a tyrant. If the green MEME does not have a healthy dose of blue, the need for equality can degenerate to the point where all ideas, even pathological ones, must be acknowledged as equal to every other belief.

As evolution proceeds to higher levels, it is essential that the evolving organism understand the process and be actively engaged in its own healthy development. This sounds quite ordinary and simple but is, in actuality, extraordinary and requires great effort and practice. In his book, *A Brief History of Everything*,[17] Wilber describes what he calls the secret impulse of evolution. He tells us that Aristotle first pointed out all of the lower is in the higher but not all of the higher is in the lower, which is what invariably establishes hierarchy or holarchy. Cells contain molecules, but not vice versa. Molecules contain atoms, but not vice versa. Sentences contain words, but not vice versa. And it is this "not vice versa" that establishes a hierarchy, a holarchy, an order of increasing wholeness.

Yet in our world so obsessed with green MEME political correctness, any suggestion of a hierarchy, of one level being higher than another, immediately brings accusations of patriarchal dominance, fascist ideology, and other assorted diabolical intentions. The simple truth is that the wholes depend on the parts. If all water were destroyed in the universe, this would not destroy the component elements of hydrogen and oxygen. A higher degree of wholeness does not signify any moral, political, or sociological superiority, but merely a different developmental sequence.

The size of something is often confused with its depth. In an evolutionary context, every succeeding level transcends, or goes beyond but includes, all previous levels. Evolution creates greater depth and less span. There are more electrons than atoms, more atoms than molecules, more molecules than cells, and so on throughout the universe. Although it may appear that bigger is better, the truth is that less is more from a developmental standpoint. One human being is more, has greater depth, than the sum of all of her component parts, which have much greater span. This can be particularly deceiving regarding human consciousness because we put so much trust in what we perceive physically, yet the full depth of human experience is only realized when we explore our deeper levels of emotional, mental, and spiritual existence.

This explanation applies precisely to the diagram of evolution presented in the Great Nest of Being. Evolution proceeds from lower to higher, from the physical to the astral to the mental to the soul to the spirit. Each level includes and transcends its predecessor, yet at each succeeding level the span decreases with increasing depth. For our discussion of the different levels of money, we start with physical money. We then develop emotions and feelings about money that become intertwined with the physical aspect of money. As we work through our deep-set feelings regarding money, we begin to develop a deeper mental appreciation for money and money ceases to be dominated by emotion, but also gains an abstract mental quality that greatly expands the uses to which we can apply money's energy. Deeper still is the soul of money. Each succeeding level of money supersedes and transcends the preceding level. As our sense of money goes to greater depth, the span gets smaller and smaller.

Take away any abstract ideas or emotional feelings regarding money, and physical money still remains. Yet if all physical money were obliterated, nothing would remain to feel or consider regarding money. For that reason it is important to understand the absolute importance of each aspect, especially how each aspect relates to the others.

As we live and learn throughout life, there is a course of development, or an evolution, that we experience. The pursuit of or lack of abundance of money is a primary aspect of life that encompasses much of our conscious attention. How and why we relate to it, therefore, is a vital topic for all of us. More important still is to come to an understanding of how and why we as individuals do or do not relate to money in a balanced manner that enables us to obtain the financial and personal goals we seek along our evolutionary path.

In succeeding chapters, we will see how different colors are intricately interwoven with each of the different levels of money consciousness. Before we do so, it is important that we differentiate the color descriptions we will use from those we explained in the Spiral Dynamics color scheme, which were developed as a handier reference than the letter codes Clare Graves originally applied to the various MEMES in his Levels of Existence. Beck and Cowen decided Grave's reference was cumbersome and developed the following color code for the eight levels:

Beige: savanna grasslands
Purple: royal color of tribal chiefs and monarchs
Red: hot blooded emotions
Blue: sky, heavens, true blue
Orange: radiating energy of steel in an industrial furnace
Green: green politics, forests, and ecological consciousness
Yellow: solar power and alternative technologies
Turquoise: color of the oceans and the earth as seen from space

We can readily see how using color associations greatly simplified discussion of the different MEMES. Yet there is nothing in the selection of each color more than a form of relative association. Substitute another color with similar characteristics and the system works just as well.

In our case, the colors representing the different levels of money are not chosen from some applied association. Each color comes from the highest monadic levels and emanates from the unmanifest into the manifest. When we say that blue is the color of the astral plane and water the defining physical element of the astral, this is based upon the specific vibrations, qualities, aspects, virtues, power, force, and energy of that color. Our test for this assertion will be our experience as we learn how to use the various colors in our understanding of money. This does not detract from the color code of Spiral Dynamics, as long as we remember to differentiate the colors of the MEMEs from the colors of the different levels of money consciousness. There will be some crossover because many of the associative aspects chosen for the MEMEs reflect some of the spiritual aspects of a color. For example, the blue MEME is a level recognized by an emphasis on hierarchical control, strict laws, and subservient obedience. This MEME is associated with periods such as the medieval age and with political and social structures that honor these aspects. In our discussion of blue in connection to the astral plane, we would say that these MEMEs operate on a low to mid level on the astral and are dominated by intense emotions.

As the evolutionary process unfolds and we develop faculties in the mental plane, the orange MEME emerges. The orange MEME is associated with the enlightenment and the emergence of the individual. In our discussion, however, the color necessary to fully activate and use the mental plane is not primarily orange, but yellow.

We can express the holarchy of any holon through the Four Quadrants model Wilber developed. The quadrants are the parts of two intersecting lines forming an axis. The two upper quadrants are considered individual and the two lower quadrants collective, whereas the left-hand quadrants are interior and the right-hand quadrants exterior.

INDIVIDUAL interior

INDIVIDUAL exterior

COLLECTIVE interior

COLLECTIVE exterior

Four Quad Graphic

All change and growth in our evolution begins within the individual interior functions and is then expressed through the individual exterior. As the individual interior functions are expressed in the exterior, they enter and affect the collective interior and are finally manifested in the collective exterior. With this in mind, to manifest our money consciousness we will:

1. Focus on our interior as individuals and how we can first balance our understanding of money within, and then see how that consciousness can manifest in our exterior lives.

2. We will do the same thing with the collective interior consciousness.

3. Finally, we will focus on manifesting money consciousness in a positive manner for the good of the exterior collective.

It may seem daunting to implement such an ambitious effort, but every journey begins with a single step. If you are diligent and dedicated and approach this challenge with humility and humor, you will find the process to be extremely rewarding and the most fun you could ever imagine. Playfulness is required in this game. In the following chapters, you may experience new ideas that differ from your familiar ideas or beliefs. There is no need to accept or reject any new idea—just experience it. To have fun, we must learn how to pretend and play, to let our imaginations run free as children do, and let our visions be our guide.

Sometimes we must move out of our mundane levels of consciousness and permit ourselves the adventure of traveling through time and space. Before you dismiss this idea as irrational or simply inconsequential, think of how you spend at least one third of your existence—asleep. Are you less of yourself when you are not fully awake? Do you dream? Do those dreams sometimes seem real?

Imagine or visualize this: On ancient Atlantis gathered on a beautiful plane overlooking the western shore in a sheltered grove of long forgotten kakokie trees, the teacher, Amatamaji, sits with her students. Let us fall back, as in a dream but with full clarity, to those days of mythic glory and transcendence before the understanding of the divine began to fade and that glorious civilization sank into the ocean of oblivion. In succeeding chapters we have the opportunity to make this journey through time and space. We will see the answers the wise teacher of Atlantis, Amatamaji, gives in response to questions from her student, Baraja.

5

The Temple of Golden Wisdom

*B*araja awoke from his reveries with a start. He glanced quickly to the bright sun and realized he would need to hurry. He did not want to be late. Today he would begin his studies with the High Master of the temple, Amatamaji. Baraja had served in the Temple of Golden Wisdom for two hundred years, and he felt quite proud that within such a short time he had earned the right to study with the high teacher.

Baraja was only one thousand years old, middle age for an Atlantean, but young for the high honor of working with the select group of Amatamaji's close students, the Light Group. He had no idea how old the wise old master was. It was said that she knew of the earliest days of Atlantis, when the first ones had arrived on Earth from the home planets and had studied the ancient wisdom of the Lemurians, the long-forgotten race of beings who lived on this planet before the rise of Atlantis. He thought that must be foolish talk because the calendar of Atlantis showed the great land had existed for over twenty generations, nearly twenty thousand years.

Well, he thought, she must be at least 6,000 years old. Even for an Atlantean, that was an old age indeed. She did not look it. He had seen her many times, but usually only during the great high holiday of Wesak or the other sacred times, when all of the many schools of the temple gathered to celebrate the most holy time of the year when the powerful Light Rays came to the earth from the great celestial cities. He thought her the most beautiful being he had ever seen. She was not beautiful in any traditional sense and, besides, beauty was a hallmark of all Atlantean women. She was tiny, standing less than five feet with waist-long, jet-black hair that she always wore bundled, but her sky-blue eyes could pierce like a thunderbolt and her calm serenity was legendary.

Baraja glanced again to the sky and hoped he would not be late and have those powerful eyes turn on him in quiet reproach. The Temple of Golden Wisdom was grand beyond belief and stretched along the majestic ocean shore for miles outside Tamron, the great capital city of Atlantis. The midday sun was rebounding off the hundreds of temple domes that designated the many different temple schools. Baraja was himself a respected elder of the Great Blue Brotherhood, one of the most prominent of the various orders. Yet there was no higher honor than to be asked to attend to Amatamaji.

The weather was beautiful, as it usually was on Atlantis. Although the frequent rain provided a lush environment for the abundant flowers and plants that nourished the inhabitants, it was gentle and warm, as was the temperature. Baraja rushed past an array of the beautiful crystals that served as the energy source for the entire continent. These crystals, thousands of feet tall and many colored, were transported on the spaceships with the original Atlanteans and came from the home planets, high pure mental planets on higher planes, such as Amatamaji's home planet Coldor, and Re-aka. He always marveled at how they seemed to float, projecting their powerful rays down. They had been strategically placed throughout the land, connected by a power grid that would provide an unlimited energy source.

Baraja, worried he would be late, considered teleporting. Atlanteans frequently teleported, a common technique most learned before their hundredth birthday. But entering such an auspicious event as his first lesson with the High Master in such a mundane fashion would not be appropriate. Baraja prided himself on his physical prowess and had earned many awards at the centennial games for his running, a skill he would use now.

Baraja, breathless after his run, balanced his energies and calmly entered the Garden of Atbar just as the temple bells sounded. Amatamaji sat upon a cushioned chair surrounded by about twenty students. She was robed in a shimmering gown of pale blue that glowed with a faint pinkish hue. Baraja took the last seat beside the Master, as she quietly said, "Welcome, my friends. It is an honor for me to have the opportunity to spend some time with you. We shall meet here each week at the same time and speak of whatever your hearts desire. Do you have any questions?"

The students looked at each other with sidelong glances, each a bit timid to be the first. Baraja took a deep breath and spoke. "What was there in the beginning of time?"

"In the beginning all was Spirit," Amatamaji answered. "Souls were then created and individualized. These souls, blended with Spirit, eventually became discontented because they failed to understand the energies that composed the whole of Creation. To correct this, the High God and the seven original high, supreme and majestic creators conceived the different planes of experience, awareness, understanding, and energy. Once the lower planes and the different universes and planets were completed, souls one by one chose to leave their perfectly blended state of consciousness in order to experience the different energies throughout Creation. This decision offered them an opportunity to learn about Creation in its entirety. The souls began to involute, that is they descended into form and matter, into the different planes and incarnate on the planets.

"The soul planes were created to allow the souls to experience spiritual en-ergies. On these levels, each soul was offered the opportunity to grow into a state of knowing regarding the various Universal Laws. Planes five through twelve housed all of the spiritual energies as well as those beings who were to assist the souls in their evolutionary return to their original blended state. These beings, or Masters, were souls who already had mastered the spiritual energies within the different planes, and who agreed to teach and guide the evolving souls. In this way, they assisted the souls in their efforts to be reunited with Spirit.

"Planets were created to correspond with the spiritual planes and energies so that those souls who wished to live in an environment of spiritual energy could eventually earn the right to live and study there. The ascension or return to God is called evolution. Each soul eventually returns, or evolves back to God, discovering and outwardly manifesting the soul's true God-nature."

"But we are not all in the spirit," Baraja said.

Amatamaji smiled. "As these souls involuted into the lower realms, their vibrations tended to become increasingly dense. It became more and more difficult for the souls to remember the beauty and peace of the higher levels, when they were surrounded by the more dense vibrations of the lower realms. They developed a sense of separateness and a distinct individuality. They also developed their own unique personalities while existing in their lower bodies on the lower planets. The individuality was called the higher self and the personality of the physical, astral, and mental bodies became the lower self.

"Initially these two were blended, but as the souls continued to incarnate and separate themselves in awareness from the higher vibrations of Creation, the higher and lower selves separated. Souls began to think of themselves not in terms of their spiritual heritage, but in terms of their individuality and their personality. This sense of separateness eventually brought about a conscious lack of recognition of the spiritual realms, which became the rule rather than the exception.

"The souls' original purpose for incarnating was to learn, grow, evolve and become more aware of all the components and energies within creation. After a number of incarnations, however, the rift between the higher and lower selves and the continued separation from the spiritual aspects of life caused the majority of souls to forget their original purpose."

"What is our purpose?" Baraja asked.

Amatamaji answered his question by posing some of her own. "What is man? What is woman? What kind of a being are they? The answer is that man and woman are spiritual beings who live in a physical body to undergo some of the experiences necessary to enable them to evolve. As man's lower instincts, drives, needs, and desires are satisfied, he becomes aware of those that exist on higher levels. He is generally able to establish a physical, emotional, mental, and spiritual sense of well-being for himself and those he cares about and is responsible for, by satisfying some or all of these.

"Man eventually began to develop his thinking and reasoning powers. In doing so, he gained the ability to analyze his actions prior to enacting them. This ability gave rise to a sense of morality, although morality, like perfection, is also relative. As he continues to evolve, his intuition developed and ultimately became the true foundation of morality in its highest sense. Man was created in the image of God and in the likeness of the universe, which means he possesses all of the elements including the ether or God-element. He has a soul and thus is capable of transcending the limitations of the lower realms and experiencing the freedom that results from gaining access to the pure, spiritual realms."

"I understand I have a physical body, but what do you mean when you speak of our other bodies?" Baraja asked.

"As souls chose to experience and to master the energies of the lower planes, they took on a polarity of male or female, those being the electric and magnetic principles within nature. To experience and work within these denser energy vibrations and vibratory frequencies, souls had to have protective coverings or "armors" known as sheaths, vehicles, or bodies.

"When souls inhabit a certain plane, they carry with them a suitable body for working within that particular plane of existence. When living in the physical, the soul possesses bodies from dense to refined. Among these are the physical body, the astral body, the mental body, and the soul body. Stated briefly, the astral or emotional body feels, desires, wants, and imagines. The mental body thinks and visualizes. The soul body perceives and knows.

"As souls first involuted into the lower planes of vibration, they worked their way down in a gradual manner that allowed them to get used to these new and different energies. Souls live many incarnations, first experiencing life on spiritual planets, then on mental planets, then gradually descending to astral, and eventually to physical planets and their corresponding planes. Once souls reach the physical plane they have completed their involution. The evolutionary process is the gradual advancement of the soul from the physical levels back up to the highest spiritual levels.

"The four basic energy or vibratory frequencies that have just been discussed are attuned to realms or planes that correspond to them in vibration. They are the physical, astral, mental, and spiritual. There are also four major bodies in which you function on the planes mentioned above: your physical body, your astral body, which serves as the seat of the emotions, your mental body, through which the mind functions, and your spiritual body, which encompasses the soul and spirit. The development of these lower bodies—the physical, astral, and mental bodies, which are known as the personality triad—is integral and is a prerequisite to the soul body's growth and development. All of our bodies are connected or linked, and each of these bodies is an integral part of the being we call self. We know the personality triad as the lower self and the causal, soul, and spirit bodies as the higher self."

"What do you mean when you say plane of existence?" Baraja asked.

"The highest levels within Creation are called the God levels. Below are the monadic levels and below these are the spiritual or soul planes. All energy possesses a particular color, sound, tone, note, rhythm, and vibratory frequency. Spiritual energy manifests through your soul or spiritual body and functions on high frequency levels of vibration, which the Masters refer to as the soul planes.

"The level or major plane below the spiritual or soul planes is the mental plane, which is denser and slower in vibratory frequency. The major plane or dimension below the mental plane and the one that is still denser and slower in vibration is known as the astral or emotional plane. The major plane below the astral is the one that is the densest and slowest of all possible vibrations within Creation. This plane is the physical plane of existence. The physical, astral, and mental planes are known as the lower planes within Creation.

"The mental plane was created to house all of the mental energies. Souls who wished to experience these energies to learn to control the vehicle of mental experience, the mental body, and all of the mind's phases, were allowed to work and study on the mental plane. They often accomplished mastery of this level while living on mental planets.

"Your mental body exists on the mental plane where it expresses thoughts and ideas and uses the visualization process. Once the energy decreases to an even lower level of vibration, it becomes astral, or psychic, energy that functions through your astral body by means of the imagination, emotions, desires, and feelings. On this level, you feel intuition from the higher realms, as well as thoughts from the mental plane, through the senses of your astral body, to the extent that this vehicle is developed enough and receptive to them. Many individuals receive psychic impressions and desires received through one's feelings or astral senses.

"This is the realm that provides man with the means by which he can establish the motivation to live, grow, and evolve. Without the feelings, emotions, and desires that are expressed on the astral plane, man would not possess the incentive he needs to enact the thoughts he has created and, thus, would be unable to manifest what he desires in the physical.

"The astral plane and astral planets were created to house psychic, emotional, and sexual energies. The astral body was created as a vehicle in which these energies could be experienced. Those who wished to incarnate in an astral body and study in this type of environment were allowed to go to astral planets. They involuted from the blended state of spirit and took on a mental body and an astral body to experience this aspect of Creation.

"The physical plane and physical planets were created for those who truly desired to experience and master the whole of Creation. Souls could then involute and experience all energies, and then evolve back to the perfected state of God-consciousness. By choosing to incarnate on the physical plane, souls could potentially gain control over their physical, astral, mental, and soul bodies and, in so doing, could accomplish the long and difficult process of mastering the accompanying energies to one degree or another. The process of mastering these energies is indeed a long and difficult one accomplished over many lifetimes."

Baraja posed another question. "You have spoken of the evolved Masters who help those of us in the physical to develop spiritually. Are there other beings that support us?"

"Some beings of an evolution parallel to ours who decided not to descend and who did not, as yet, choose to leave these higher planes, are known as angels. These beings have instead chosen to remain in the higher planes to help their brother and sister souls who have descended to experience, master, and know God's creation. Souls can decide if and when they will make their descent from the higher levels. If angels decide to descend or involute into Creation's denser energy vibrations, they would no longer be considered angels, but would be regarded as evolving souls who have chosen the path of spiritual mastery, experiencing and eventually returning to the higher planes and to God.

"When we have worked our way back to God by mastering these high, pure energy states and planes, we become what are known as God-conscious Beings and High Spiritual Masters. In a sense, we are all prodigal sons and daughters returning home—to God and to the higher planes from whence we first came.

"As souls descend into form, they leave their spirits—that is energies of different quality and quantity—and the monad, the higher God-consciousness, with God in the high akashic, or spiritual, ethers. The monad is known as the Spark of God, although it is truly much more than that, and Spirit is the individualized expression of God.

"Angels possess a soul. They are neither male nor female, even though they work with both the electric and magnetic polarities. Consequently, they can take any form they desire. They could, for instance, take the form of a human being, yet they have never lived in a physical body on Earth. Their primary purpose for existence, and this is especially true of the guardian angels who watch over and protect you as long as you live on the physical plane, is to help mankind grow and evolve.

"That is all we have time for today. Think about what you have learned and perhaps, Baraja, next time you will share some time with your fellow students." She smiled mischievously and, although he knew she was only kidding him, he blushed slightly and grinned.

Well, he thought quietly to himself, they better speak up. Baraja had just spent his first time with the Master and he wanted more.

PART II

Finding Your MoneyForce

6
The Colors of Money

"Mere color, unspoiled by meaning, and unallied with definite form,
can speak to the soul in a thousand different ways."
—Oscar Wilde

As noted in the introduction, the purpose of this book is to provide you with the tools you need to balance your relationship with money. Although it is useful to learn about the different planes of money, review some historical perspective, and hear observations about money, the only way to internalize what we talk about in this book is to have a personal experience. In this chapter, we will discuss money and color, how you can use your personal power, force, and energy in your relationship with money, and a technique to activate your MoneyForce to better achieve your personal, financial, and spiritual goals.

Money and Color

When we speak about the colors of money we are not referring to the color of any specific currency. For our purposes, the color of money refers to the vibratory frequency of different colors and how they affect our physical bodies, our emotions, and our thoughts. Everyone is aware of color but, because we are constantly in the midst of color, we lose sight of how deeply we are affected by the different energies emanating from the spectrum. On Valentine's Day we send our loved ones cards in the color that most evokes feelings of love, pink. When we wish to select a soothing, comforting color for a room in which we wish to relax and reflect in quiet meditation, we often choose a shade of pale blue.

The power of these colors does not originate from some mental construct we have created or purely as a result of societal convention. It comes from the highest spiritual levels and is a direct connection between all planes of consciousness. The energy of the different colors resonates with our astral, mental, and soul vibrations and blends us with those levels of consciousness. To activate our MoneyForce, we must be conscious of how the colors work on the different levels and learn how we can use colors to better achieve our conscious desires and goals.

Energy, Power, and Force

In a dictionary, these words are often used to describe the other and are used in language almost interchangeably. To master your MoneyForce, it is necessary to understand the difference between these three energies, develop the ability to feel the difference, and increase the capacity and faculty of consciously applying each one in the appropriate amount and way in different circumstances. When used with a capital E, Energy signifies the combined integration of each aspect of the total including power, energy, and force. The energy contained within Energy is a part of the whole. Energy contains the full dimension of all of the distinct aspects.

When speaking of energy think of it as the source activator, the fuel that initiates, engenders, activates, and vitalizes. We feel this every day when our blood sugar level lowers, as we get hungry and our energy wanes. After eating, assuming we have consumed something healthy and nutritious, we feel revitalized and energized, with greater physical strength, emotional stability, and mental clarity. When working with higher consciousness, the ability to obtain and direct abundant positive energy is essential to accomplishing any goal. If there is an essential ingredient in your soul cookbook, it is energy.

When we speak of any Energy, it is of paramount importance to understand and state clearly that we are addressing only pure positive energy, power, and force. Only these will raise your levels of consciousness and contribute to the higher evolution of your soul.

If energy is the fuel, power is the enhancer that expands and compounds for greater growth, strength, and ability. To use an analogy with electricity, if energy is voltage, power is amplitude.

For those who prefer an automotive example, think of energy as the horsepower and power as the supercharger that greatly increases the output of the engine.

Force provides the focus, concentration, actualization, and realization of the potential found in energy and power. Consider a military analogy. Individual soldiers possess great energy and potential, but bound together in increasingly larger units they increase their power. Power alone is difficult to control and maximize in potential unless a strong leader concentrates the fighting units into a potent force and guides them.

In the same manner, an individual needs to recognize the different energies and potential of energy, power, and force and learn how to use these in her life. In many cases, the most important lesson is that quality, not quantity, is much more important and effective when working with Energy. This is a case where less is often more, and one of the greatest challenges in working with Energy is to learn how to apply subtle energy, power, and force.

Magnetic and Electric

Earlier we saw a long set of apparent contradictions that are part of the human condition. We spend a good part of our lives attempting to reconcile the duality of the incongruities we experience daily. Philosophers and religious leaders have dedicated much of their lives to attempting to reconcile how such contractions can exist in the presence of a divine, loving God. It is a perplexing dilemma.

There are no easy answers, but a good starting point is to recognize the most elemental and primal fact in positive creation: the existence of magnetic and electric. We are all aware of the scientific concepts and the practical applications we experience every day. Magnetic energy is the root of our planetary polarization and is applied in diverse technology. Electric energy has become the world's most indispensable modern energy source.

We experience these energies in our physical existence, but these manifestations are only an indication of the true importance and the immense scale that these forces exert. They are the Yin and Yang, complementary yet opposing forces that are at the root of all creation. Understanding this fact, and developing the means to feel and control magnetic and electric energy, is essential to higher evolution.

In simple terms, electric is the positive charge to a magnetic negative charge. This should not be confused with positive and negative in a moral context. All energy we choose to experience and work with is only positive, including all magnetic energy. Magnetic is negatively charged in that it is the polar opposite of electric; if electric is the activator then magnetic is the receptor. Our bodies carry electric and magnetic energy, with our right side primarily electric and our left side primarily magnetic.

Meditation

Meditation goes back to the earliest days of mankind. Often when we hear the word, meditation we think of eastern religions and awkward sitting positions. Sometimes meditation is associated with certain cultural or political beliefs. This is unfortunate, because everyone meditates in one form or another every day. Any time we concentrate on something, we begin to experience a sort of meditation. The depth of the experience and the result of the concentration depend on the focus of our will, intent, and attention. When we focus on an external object or a desired external physical or emotional outcome, our experience is different than if our concentration is directed internally and the desired outcome is not physically or emotionally self-centered. For example, prayer is a form of meditation that many people are aware of and practice. Certainly a heartfelt prayer for the health and well-being of others is a different experience from the perfunctory prayer before the attempted free throw in a basketball game.

Meditation is a way to concentrate that can help us open to deep, cleansing, and pleasurable inner awareness. It is the heart of prayer and our most natural activity as human beings. Although at first meditating may seem difficult and uncomfortable, think of the daunting prospect you faced as a child when your mom or dad decided it was time to remove the training wheels from your bicycle. You may have had a tumble or two, but what a feeling when, amidst your protestations, you realized that Dad had not been holding on for the last fifty feet.

The primary obstacle to meditation is that we think too much about so many reasons why we can't meditate. Quiet things down a bit, relax, and just let good old Mother Nature take over, and I think you will find that meditation is indeed the easiest and most natural human activity. Like riding a bicycle, once you learn how, you never forget, no matter how much time lapses between sessions.

I am going to suggest some practical ways for you to meditate to achieve whatever positive goals you may have. These are not religious in any way and will not conflict with any personal religious beliefs you may hold. Just as we need to exercise to keep our bodies healthy, these techniques are designed to keep our astral, mental, and soul bodies in good shape.

The first step in practicing any of the exercises throughout this book is to learn some basics of meditation. If you currently practice meditation or have practiced a technique in the past, please feel free to use it.

Exercise 1: Bringing in Energies

1. Close your eyes and mentally state: "I am bringing magnetic energy into my body."

2. Imagine or visualize that you are bringing a pale blue ball into your body, starting at the top of your head and bringing it down along the left side of your body through your head, into your shoulders and back, into your chest and stomach, into your hips and thighs, and finally exiting your feet.

3. Mentally state: "I am bringing electric energy into my body."

4. Imagine or visualize that you are bringing a bright red ball of color into your body, starting at your head and bringing it down your entire right side as you did before.

5. When you have finished, with your eyes still closed, hold your hands shoulder-width apart with your elbows bent, and then slowly bring your hands together palms facing each other until they are about one inch from touching.

What do you feel? You may experience a sensation similar to when you take two magnets and rotate them from their magnetic attraction. It is impossible for them to come together. Though not as dramatic, as your hands come closer you may sense a unique energy emanating from each that is similar, yet distinct, and that these two energies, electric and magnetic, attract and repel each other. They may seem to create their own energy zone between your palms. This is called electro-magnetic energy.

Exercise 2: Tree Hugging

1. Find a secluded wooded area, preferably with some larger trees you find especially attractive.

2. Find a tree that "speaks" to you and sit quietly under it for several minutes.

3. Quiet your mind and body by slowly bringing in several deep breaths and exhaling just as slowly.

4. When you feel you have slowed down your mind and emotions,

slowly stand and move your right hand gradually closer to the tree at chest level.

5. As your hand gets to within about three inches of the tree, what do you feel? Do you feel a tingling or other sensation in your hand?

6. Now try this with your left hand. Do you experience the same sensation or is it different?

7. Take both hands and place them on the tree for several minutes. Try to keep your mind still and focus all attention solely on the tree and your presence with the tree.

Many people are amazed with their first "tree hugging" experience—and perhaps a bit embarrassed. We shouldn't be. The plant kingdom is an indispensable part of our biosphere and, because we are absolutely dependant on plants for our existence, we should not be surprised at our ability to communicate with them.

All souls are charged either electric or magnetic and this charge determines the principal path of involution and evolution for that soul. Magnetic souls will incarnate primarily in female bodies and electric souls as males. No, males are not all from Mars and women from Venus. Woman can indeed manifest intense electric energy when necessary and men have tremendous powers of receptivity. It is not a question of strength versus gentleness. Electric energy can be quite strong, sudden, and overpowering, like a lightening bolt, but it is difficult to sustain and direct. In contrast, magnetic forces, often less overtly recognized than the electric, are actu-ally stronger because they generate more self-sustaining, long-term energy. They can be directed in a manner that produces stronger, more sustained outcomes.

Ideally, we can develop the ability to use magnetic and electric energy, power, and force with the recognition of when to apply each, at what level of intensity, and with complete control. In most cases, more energy is not better and can often be counterproductive to the task at hand. Remember, "Less is more" when dealing with electric and magnetic Energy.

7
The Way of Balance

*F*or the past week, since his first lesson with Amatamaji, Baraja's mind had been swirling with all of the information he had received. It seemed like the more he thought about what he had learned the more frustrated and uncertain he was about how to proceed. The week had passed in a blur. He was excited. He knew he was on the edge of learning something vital for fulfilling his life's purpose, but he had many more questions than answers and sometimes felt like he was going to burst. He could hardly wait until the next group session, and almost before Amatamaji had settled her pale yellow robes as she sat down, he blurted out, "I would like to meditate because I want to quiet my mind and be more focused in my life, but I am not sure what meditation is or even how I should meditate."

"The dividing line between meditation and concentration is slight," Amatamaji began, "yet there is a distinct difference between the two. Concentration is a mental exercise, whereas meditation is a spiritual exercise. In concentration, you gain conscious control of the mind, single-pointedly focusing on and holding one particular object or thought. During this exercise, you maintain complete awareness of every mental effort you make—whether it is the effort to focus on the specific thought or object or to push out intruding ones.

"In meditation, the necessity to concentrate on consciously controlling the thought processes no longer exists. It is an exercise in which you still the mind to experience a harmonized spiritual state of active receptivity. In this state of consciousness, energies you need can flow from the higher planes and be received in an equally pure condition in the lower realms.

"The purpose of meditation is threefold. Meditation helps you harmonize your higher mental faculties, enables you to learn to consciously take control and dominate the lower self—the physical, astral, and mental bodies—and ultimately allows you to blend these bodies in perfect union with the higher self. Your higher mental faculties must be harmonized before you can transcend your inner, dormant spiritual qualities and achieve a higher state of consciousness. You must acquire by your own efforts the greater awareness that exists within the spiritual realms. Only by doing so, can you ultimately merge all of your bodies into the one all-knowing God consciousness.

"Meditation is the art of uniting the soul and all other parts of your being with the spirit, or God. When the soul reincarnates in a bodily form, it gradually loses its own identity and begins to identify with the physical consciousness and its limitations. The purpose of meditation is to gradually reawaken the soul—or soul-consciousness—until the physical consciousness can recall its divine, immortal nature and origin. As the soul consciously progresses into ever-higher levels of awakening and awareness, it experiences a greater sense of understanding and peace, which eventually begins to manifest on all levels of consciousness.

"Through this technique you will ultimately be able to enter the higher planes, which offer knowledge and wisdom rarely found in the lower realms. You will discover universal laws as yet unknown to most. When you learn and gradually apply them, you will alter many of your present values. Once you become aware of your inner faculties, you will want to develop them. The higher truths you begin to acquire in this process contain pure energies that cannot flow freely into an impure body. You will eventually find yourself attempting to live a purer life increasingly attuned to your new understanding."

"How do I meditate?" Baraja asked.

"You need to apply some of the basic principles involved in relaxation and concentration: the best time—dawn, midday, and dusk. The area—a special place you have set aside for your spiritual exercises, facing north if possible. The position—spine straight, hands and legs crossed right over left in whichever way is most comfortable for you. You should be relaxed but not so much that you fall asleep. Then you will follow these steps:

1. You will need to become completely relaxed. Find a restful place where you can lie down.

2. Allow your body to go limp with your arms resting comfortably at your side and your legs approximately twelve inches apart with your feet turned slightly outward.

3. Close your eyes, release all sense of strain and turmoil, then begin to relax every cell and tissue in your body.

4. Feel a tingling sensation of peace flood your entire being, beginning

at the top of your head. Allow this sensation to slowly flow to your eyes, ears, brain, face, back of your head, neck, shoulders, arms, hands, and fingers. As you gradually relax the organs, tissues, and cells in your back, chest, abdomen, thighs, calves, and feet, continue to feel the tingling sensation of calmness in the various parts of your body while you are individually relaxing them.

5. When you have worked with your entire body, return to the top of your head and allow a beautiful pale blue light of peaceful stillness to flow from that point throughout your body and out the bottom of your feet.

"You will feel completely relaxed when you have learned to master this technique, so much so that at times you will consciously have to overcome the tendency to fall asleep. This is only natural and may require several practice sessions before you are able to exercise your will not to fall asleep or want to go to sleep. You will eventually be able to maintain this peaceful state for a brief time. When you feel you are ready to go on to the next technique, gradually sit up, arise, and go to the place you chose to conduct your spiritual exercises. Then follow these steps:

1. Sit down quietly, close your eyes, roll them slightly upward, and focus them towards the point between the eyebrows where the third eye is located. Try not to strain or cross your eyes. Although this position may seem uncomfortable at first, you will gradually become accustomed to it. Relax your body again.

2. Repeat the following to yourself, three or four times: "I am not the body. I only exist in the body."

3. Turn your attention to the mind. Visualize yourself as an observer and the mind as a vast ocean in which waves of thoughts flow gently in and out. As the thoughts roll in, observe them and then allow them to flow back to the ocean from whence they came. Gradually allow the mind you are observing to become as calm and still as the ocean is on a clear and beautiful day. To achieve this will take practice and patience, but when you reach the state of consciousness in which you can still your mind and control the thoughts that enter and leave it, you will be prepared to begin the next technique.

"This exercise involves allowing one object or thought to be the center of attention in your mind. You can focus on a multi-colored flower, a lovely tree, or a pastoral scene—one that you have actually seen or one that you imagine. The steps are as follows," Amatamaji said as she began to enumerate them:

1. In an effortless manner, allow many different thoughts concerning the subject you have selected to gently flow into your mind. In a few seconds you will notice other thoughts or trains of thought, totally unrelated to the subject you have selected, demanding your attention. Gently push out the intruding thoughts and refocus your attention on your original scene or object. At first you will probably have to gently push away a number of intruding thoughts, to allow space for the thoughts you want to flow in to enter your consciousness.

2. The purpose of this technique is to learn to single-pointedly focus your attention on a specific thought or thoughts to prevent outside thoughts from interrupting. When you can maintain your chosen train of thought without interruption for approximately three minutes, you will have mastered this exercise and can go on to the next one.

"All of the above techniques will help prepare your consciousness for meditation. This particular exercise is especially important because it will help you attune yourself to that state in which you are actively receptive to the divine within. Relax completely and gently push any intruding thoughts away, eventually blanking your mind. Although it will take time, once you have achieved this goal you will have mastered the basic prerequisites necessary to learn to meditate effectively."

Baraja spent the next week practicing the meditation techniques he had learned. At first he grew restless after a few minutes and other times his thoughts seemed to rush uncontrolled through his mind. By the end of the week, however, he could sit quietly for almost an hour. He felt a tranquil joy when he stilled his mind, and he noticed he was becoming aware of different colors that passed before his mind's eye as he meditated. At the next lesson he inquired of the Master, "You have spoken about the power of color. What is the meaning of all the different colors?"

"The colors contain the essence of energies that come from the highest levels down through the planes. It is necessary to understand and use colors wisely to grow and fulfill your life's purpose," she replied.

"How can we use our understanding of the colors to find balance in our life?" Amatamaji decided this would be the time to introduce her students to the relationship of color and energy. "Once you have understanding, you can bring the colors into your different bodies to help convey the energies of those colors into your own being. All of the colors will be electric and magnetic. These aspects will enable you to absorb self-assurance, a sense of inner as well as outer joy, a desiring of peace. It will help bring a balance of mental enlightenment, a sense of freedom from the limitations of your mind, be it your conscious, subconscious, or unconscious. It will be a color of freedom and elimination. It will help you eliminate the old and absorb the new and the good, to see the good, to raise your levels of consciousness, to gain a new understanding by being able to mentally function in a new place, and to expand and help figure out what is wrong and how it can be righted. Let's look at the different colors."

"Red represents divine will, gratitude, caring, truthfulness, compassion, forgiveness, letting go of old ideas, persistence, courage and a sense of good will to all.

"Orange represents love, wisdom, constructiveness, enthusiasm, enterprise, as well as the ability to flow with nature and absorb love into your hearts and minds.

"The highest expression of yellow is divine intellect. It is considered to be one of the happiest colors of the spectrum because it creates positive force for clear thinking, for decision making, for studying, etcetera. It leads us to higher inspiration and illumination of ideas. Other parts of yellow are expressed as praise, clear thinking, logic, ingenuity, the ability to discern and understand quickly, to be decisive, optimistic, and to embody a clear sense of reason.

"The highest expression of green is divine balance. At the center of the physical color spectrum, green dominates: the green trees, the green plants, the giver of life here for us. It promotes growth through desire and pure harmony. There is a harmony within each tree. There is a resonance within each blade of grass. Something in your mind or body resonates every time you look down at a mound of green grass, a blended, balanced harmony and rhythm. It's almost as if rhythm and resonance and sound and balance are dancing in the air, giving off this energy. It is stimulating and soothing at the same time. It helps you laugh at yourself. Tints of green represent control—all types of control. If you do not have green in your aura or your soul, color, or personality ray somewhere, then you will have a harder time with control and self-control. Justice is also associated with the color green. Someone who judges improperly or who judges others but cannot see or judge himself would be a person who needs green.

"Pure, true humility and sympathy and empathy fall under the realm of green—sympathy a bit too much and empathy more balanced. True order is associated with green, as well as discrimination, a sense of equity, the ability to cooperate, to work within the scheme of things, and to do things in a timely manner. It is the renewal color, the perfect color for almost all types of healing. That is why in the summer, if you are sick or do not feel well, you can go out into the mountains or forests amongst the trees and pull in their energy and come back renewed.

"There are two highest expressions of blue. One is faith and the other is peace. They are both equally divine. Blue is also an expression of devotion and trustworthiness, being of service to God and mankind, inventiveness, tactfulness, and a sense of beauty. Truth and serenity are other attributes of blue. If you seek pure truth and have blue in your various colors or color spectrums, then you will be able to find that truth easier. If you do not have a lot of blue in your color rays or spectrums, then you can bring it in and desire to know the truth, the pure truth, and you will have it. Blue, pale blue, of course, is magnetic, but blue is also a color of power, just like red. All of the colors can be power colors, but blue and red can be two of the highest of the power colors.

"In its highest expression, indigo is integration and being at one with self or achieving a state of at-oneness. This is also a color for intellect, faith, and trust, trusting that you're on the right path, trusting God, trusting positive beings. Tolerance, clarity of perception, practical idealism, and a sense of unity are attributes of blue.

"I don't know anyone who doesn't need unity. Unity means being at one with your whole being, totally aligned and blended on all levels, and being at one with others as well. Indigo combines the deep blue of devotion with the purity and stabilization of the red to promote clear, logical thought and a true understanding of what life is. When indigo combines deep blue with violet, it brings in a spiritual aspect that gives you more of an understanding of what all of life is about. When it's joined by pink, it increases your ability to experience and express those energies from the highest, or the spirit, with your lower bodies. You can achieve a greater state of at-oneness and more of a lower enlightenment state by combining the violets and the pink with all the other colors I've mentioned.

"Purple is one of the true colors of devotion. It is an often-misinterpreted color. Many people think of it as representing royalty, but, in truth, it represents the higher exalted being.

"Violet in its highest expression is divine transmutation. The other attributes associated with violet and other tints of it can include pure idealism, dedication, reverence, and true self-realization—the ability to realize who you truly are as a being. Intuitiveness, alertness, and pure realization of the soul are expressions of the violet. Violet blends with red (will) and blue (truth) to transmute the lower into the higher. When you have a lower quality, let's say improper discernment or judgment, you want to transmute to a higher quality, violet will come in and join with red and blue to help you do that. These colors are always at play in your everyday life—every day of your life. The choices, the things you do, will determine how much color you have in your rays, how much color will affect you, and how much of it you need.

"The color pink represents pure love. It is the unconditional love color that will come in every time you think nice, sweet thoughts about someone. When you think negative thoughts such as "I can't do that," or "I'll never remember that lesson," you're limiting yourself and you pull away balance, you pull away green. Do not think in terms that limit you. The more you do that, the more the colors, your mind, and the ether will work against you. Always use and choose your words carefully such as, "I choose not to do this now. It is my choice."

"How do the colors work with our different bodies on the physical, astral, mental, and soul planes?" Baraja asked.

"The bodies have three auras or color spectrums. They are, from densest to most subtle, the personality rays, which can be seen astrally, the color rays, which exist from the physical up to the fifth soul plane, and the soul rays, which are found in the higher soul planes.

"The physical body is the base for the lower aura or personality rays. By looking at this lower aura and viewing the pureness of the colors, you can tell how evolved an individual is or if the person is experiencing a physical ailment. The lower aura flows in a circular motion from the mental body down to the physical and back up again. The higher auras do not flow in this way. The etheric body is a bluish-pink or a peach-blue color when it is pure and receiving pure energies. These pure energies are hard to find in etheric bodies of people living on the earth because the earth's energies are not pure.

"Red/brown is the principal color associated with the physical plane and blue with the astral plane. Yellow is the guiding color in the mental plane and violet in the soul plane. In addition to colors, certain physical elements are associated with each plane: earth with the physical, water with the astral, air with the mental, and fire with the soul plane."

This raised a question about the elements. "I often feel the power of life when I am in nature and exposed to her forces, the bare elements of earth, air, water, and fire," Baraja began. "I love to sleep on the earth, play in clear waters, breathe the mountain air, and gaze deeply into a blazing fire. Why do I feel these things?"

"The incarnating soul's astral and mental experiences in his previous lives are primarily responsible for determining the characteristics of his astral and mental bodies. His ability in the past to use the ether, fire, air, water, and earth elements also influences his physical, astral, and mental makeup. These elements will be incorporated into his various bodies to the extent he has learned to work with them, either consciously or unconsciously.

"The fire element works with the sense of sight. It produces light and luminescence through which we see life. If a person is enthusiastic, courageous, and productive, he has learned to work with the fire element and its positive qualities. On the other hand, pessimism, irritability, jealousy, a fiery temper, and, in the extreme, destructive tendencies indicate the individual either lacks or has too much of the fire element in his mental, astral, and/or physical bodies.

"The air element works with the sense of taste as well as with the mental body and its ability to think clearly. People who use their mental faculties a great deal of the time often unconsciously pull in large quantities of air element and, in the process, feel hunger. These people are often interested in the gustatory arts. If you find yourself excessively hungry, work with the elements technique to release the excess air element and balance the elements within your bodies.

"The ability to be kind, cheerful, optimistic, diligent, and independent indicates a positive use of the air element. On the other hand, too much or too little contained within an individual's various bodies would cause him to be pessimistic, easily depressed, to lack endurance, talk too much, be dishonest, or lack the ability to maintain a lasting relationship.

"The water element works with the sense of touch and feeling as well as in developing perception—knowing through feeling. If an individual has learned to work with the water element, he will be compassionate, forgiving, serene, modest, and respectable. Comprehension, devotion, meditation, the ability to give aid quickly, and a zest for life are further indications that an individual has learned to incorporate the water element into his three lower bodies. Passivity, shyness, laziness, indifference, and depression, however, result from either too little or too much of the water element.

"Perhaps one of the more beneficial elements a soul entering the physical learned to work with in the past is the earth element. Its positive qualities enable a person to be conscientious, considerate, objective, thorough, responsible, reliable, punctual, self-confident, self-assured, and firm but loving. However, if the soul has allowed its lower vehicles to become attuned to the earth element's negative qualities, the individual could be dull, untidy, lazy, tardy, unreliable, or even unscrupulous. Too little of the earth element can cause sluggishness and fatigue, impotence, a lack of sexual desire, and the inability to experience sexual fulfillment. Too much of the earth element can cause absentmindedness and an overactive sex drive.

"The elements greatly influence your astral temperament. You will benefit by focusing your attention on their positive qualities and bringing them into better balance within your bodies. You can begin to work with them now by imagining only that amount you require of the earth, water, air, and fire. Once you do this, immediately imagine the excess you have of any of these elements flowing out of your bodies into the universe. If you find yourself manifesting the negative aspects of the elements and you're unsure as to whether you possess too much or too little of one, this technique will draw in more of the element if you need it. If you already have enough of one or more of the elements, any excess will return to the universe when you push out the excess and will then provide for their harmonious interaction."

8
Physical Money, Red/Brown

"When people and nations make progress in their materialistic ambitions, they may experience some temporary improvement of mood, but it is likely to be short-lived and superficial. The sad truth is that when people feel the emptiness of their material success, or failure, they often persist in thinking more will be better, and thus continue to strive for what will never make them happier."
—Tim Kasser[18]

Introduction

Red represents will, gratitude, caring, truthfulness, and compassion. We could title this chapter "Real Money" because most people have the best understanding and the closest relationship with money—good and bad—on the physical plane. It is in the physical that we experience the most basic money need, sustenance. In this chapter we will explore our attitudes and attachment to money and learn how to control how we relate to our efforts for material success.

How We Relate to Physical Money: More or Enough.

The majority of people struggle to earn a living. In the United States and most of the developed nations, we take basic survival for granted. Yet the most destitute homeless person in the United States is probably living at a higher standard than most of the world's poorest population. This may sound harsh, but consider that the poorest beggar in the United States has access to temporary food and shelter and even begging a few dollars a day generates more income than many workers earn in the poorest third world countries. In the United States we define the poverty level as those earning under $11,880 per year, according to the 2016 Health and Human Services Poverty Statistics for a one-person family in the lower forty-eight states. This is certainly not a sum providing any level of basic comfort according to our standards, but is a huge sum in sub-Saharan Africa where the average annual income is measured in the hundreds.

This point was obvious to me during a cab ride to the airport. Our Nigerian driver was a delightful, educated, polite man with a positive attitude. Our conversation centered on his origins, family, and his desire to earn enough money in the United States to enable him to return to Nigeria to help others. When I tipped him ten dollars for a thirty-dollar fare, he did not hide his delight nor feign his appreciation. "Oh, thank you, sir, you have given me so much monies." The average income in his country is perhaps four hundred dollars per year. The ten dollars he would send home to his family represented over one week's earnings.

As much of the rest of the world knows, it does not take much money to meet the basic survival needs—food, clothing, and shelter. Much of our views on the quality of existence depend on our perspective. Most Americans would feel utterly deprived were they to experience the basic standard of living of a sub-Saharan African, whereas the African knows nothing else and is grateful for simply surviving.

Perhaps the closest I've ever come to having an experience approximating the daily experience of the poorest in the world came on a camping trip my son, who was twelve at the time, and I took in the Porcupine Mountains in the upper peninsula of Michigan. We were on the first day of a three-day hike and were about three hours into our trek along a trail next to Lake Michigan when I noticed a gathering storm. We headed for a marked campsite only to find it occupied. We scurried along the lakeshore, under a rapidly darkening sky with increasing wind, looking for a break in the thick woods.

Finally I realized our time was up. We ran into the brush, hurriedly set up our tent, and dove in just as the heavens opened up. All around us, nature was wreaking havoc. Yet, I felt such a profound sense of security and contentment as I sat in that tent with one of the people I most love. I had survived and was protecting the child who would carry on my line to the next generation. Our meager physical condition was immaterial. I could have been seated in a majestic lodge and not felt as protected.

It would be nice to say I experience this level of contentment with all my possessions, but that would be false. Most of us are conditioned by our environment and measure much of our happiness and prosperity by the extent of our physical wealth. Certainly possessions have little correlation to need and often even to want. We have these things because we can and because we live in a country that extols, and requires for its economic existence, the glory of consumerism. I possess, therefore I am.

But does money buy happiness? As the singer Sophie Tucker once said, "I have been poor and I have been rich. Rich is better." I agree, but I struggle with the question of how much is enough. More is seldom better and often leads to the malaise of the idle rich—opulent boredom and lack of purpose. The attainment of material possessions often provides a sense of well- being, but this experience is temporary. As the effect of the possession wears off, we are driven to acquire ever more in the misguided belief that more possessions will make us feel better.

The growth of our physical wealth is normal and healthy, as long as we respect the difference between enjoying the fruits of physical comfort and recognizing the benefits of sharing that wealth. If we become attached to possessing material wealth, we risk losing sight of our true life's purpose.

This contradiction regarding physical wealth prevails in many religions, especially Christianity. Much U.S. economic success can be attributed to money values, such as the Protestant work ethic, we inherited from our forbearers. Many Protestant denominations, primarily the Presbyterians and Baptists, fostered a belief in predestination, which states salvation is preordained, and no amount of good works will affect it. Only faith will allow the opportunity for eternal life. This dour perspective encouraged productivity, as many believed the appearance of earthly success was a good indication that an individual was, indeed, one of the elect.

In the _Bible_, this attitude is often contravened where most references Jesus made regarding money did not support the acquisition of wealth, but suggested it is easier to achieve spiritual goals unencumbered by the responsibilities of wealth. Perhaps the most quoted passage is from the synoptic gospels, the three that tell the same story: "It is easier for a camel to pass through the eye of a needle than for a rich man to enter the kingdom of heaven."(Matthew 19:24, Mark 10:25, and Luke 18:25). A reader today, visualizing someone attempting to pass through a sewing needle, would suspect Jesus of laying on the hyperbole. Yet an explanation that makes much more sense changes the meaning of the quote.

As written, the proscription sounds as though Jesus is saying that the mere possession of wealth is a major hindrance to eternal life. Gilbert Bowen, emeritus minister at the Kenilworth Union Church in Kenilworth, Illinois, has a different interpretation. During the time of Christ, merchants would travel from one walled town to the next during daylight. It was critical for them to reach the safety of the city each night, because they and their goods were vulnerable to robbers if they arrived after the gates were closed for the evening.

The large gates permitted the passage of heavily laden carts, horses, and camels, but once closed, the only passage into the town was via a small, easily defended doorway adjacent to the gate called the "needle." This presents the verse in an entirely different light. A merchant arriving late faced a difficult decision: if he abandoned his goods outside the city and took personal safety, he would save himself, yet most certainly lose his fortune. Conversely, if he remained outside the city with his pack animals, he faced the prospect of losing his life while defending his goods. The commentary against wealth then was not directed at possessing wealth, but rather at the attitude toward it, that of being attached to it.

If it is true we can meet the basic physical needs of existence with relatively small amounts of money, then it would appear the greatest area of preoccupation with accumulating money is based in our emotions and our various thoughts about money. The physical does not provide the locus for our higher need for money, even though it appears to be the money's pre-eminent domain because we are so dependant on our basic survival needs and spend so much of our time devoted to activities designed to earn money.

The tent surrounding my son and me during the storm met our basic shelter needs, but we would certainly find a tent as a permanent residence a physical hardship and unsatisfactory for our emotional and mental well-being. As we rise up the scale of physical affluence, the same relationship applies. A tiny one-room apartment in an inner-city ghetto is far superior to a skimpy tent, but would not compare to a two-story, four-bedroom, three-bath home in the suburbs.

This relationship supports the premise of span and depth in succeeding hierarchies. The physical realm of money has, by far, the greatest span. Everyone must confront the physical issues of money daily. Although the scope of that effort varies, depending on the economic strata of each individual, we share needs we must meet. I must have shelter, be that a humble tent in the Sahara or a sixty-thou-sand-square-foot mansion. I must feed my family whether it's one meager meal of rice and vegetables or a seven-course dinner at a five-star restaurant.

The judgment of where we want to be on that spectrum brings us into the area of subjective values. It would be easy to answer that any sane person would choose greater affluence and that would intuitively appear true, especially at the lowest levels of wealth. Yet we must be careful not to apply and project our own emotional and mental biases upon the supposition. There are Masai herdsmen in South Africa who measure wealth by the size of their herd. For them, possessing two hundred cattle may be the equivalent of living in a mansion, although they continue to reside in a tent. In the United States, a rancher with a two-hundred-head herd would probably be operating on a modest level. Similarly, a wealthy Bedouin sheik in Saudi Arabia may have access to millions of dollars of oil wealth, yet choose to live in a tent in the desert surrounded by the asset he values most, his horses and family.

During my career as a financial planner, I observed that it's not the physical possession of money that drives the intense desire for acquiring it, but the emotional and mental sense of attainment and security it represents. Often the addition of ever-greater material goods is inversely related to satisfaction.

My first car was a bare bones Datsun, and when I married we had a Toyota Corona. Those two cars provided me as much enjoyment as any form of transportation I have experienced since, probably because my only criteria for an auto at that time was to get me where I wanted to go as cheaply and efficiently as possible. Over the years we progressed through Volvos to a succession of Mercedes. I chose the Mercedes because, late one evening on a trip to southern Indiana to visit my mother, I was pushing the speed limit, going over eighty mph, when the transmission seals on our Volvo wagon overheated. We lost our transmission fluid and came to a halt. My wife and I, carrying our infant son, tramped along a desolate, cornfield-walled stretch of Highway 63 in Vermillion County, Indiana toward what resembled Tony Perkins' Victorian house on the hill in _Psycho_. Barking farm dogs heralded our approach. At that moment I vowed, if we survived the night, I would purchase the safest motorcar available. Mercedes Benz was the clear choice.

Although I told myself I was upgrading solely for altruistic reasons, providing safety for my family, I soon found that not only did I enjoy the silky smooth suspension, the ultra-quiet ride, and the cat-like quick response, but also the turn of heads and respectful looks I garnered as I tooled down the road. I secretly relished this silent homage and quiet envy because, in those days, Benz owners were not as prevalent as today. Eventually, I grew uncomfortable with the image others projected on me because I owned this particular car.

In the mid-eighties I entered a period of self-reflection. My chosen vehicle for this adventure was the newly designed Jeep Cherokee. This was prior to soccer moms across America making the Cherokee and all of the succeeding generations of SUVs ubiquitous throughout our land. Jeep ownership in those days was not the norm. The pure performance of the vehicle definitely met my needs for on- and off-road exploration, not to mention great traction on snowy Chicago roads. The most satisfaction I got from our old Jeep—our "pony" as my wife christened it—was the emotional sense I felt from owning a car that made a different statement about me than the Mercedes did.

It is the attachment to wealth, rather than its possession that most drives us, often with little real satisfaction. As I stated earlier, my clients did not regard themselves as rich. They continued to fret over the bills and their financial future, even as they appreciated their affluence. This happens because the physical has the greatest span in our lives, but it is woefully inept when it comes to our need for increased depth.

Sometimes religions will attempt to reconcile this situation by denying the physical. Christianity has often held poverty as an ideal to facilitate spiritual development. This is a grave error and leads to retardation of spiritual growth and emotional and mental health. Rather than degrade the physical, we need to acknowledge it and strive to keep a balance between our need for money and our desire for physical, emotional, mental, and spiritual gratification. We cannot allow our pursuit of money to lead to an overriding desire to possess money, to an attachment to the mere possession of material wealth. We need to be comfortable with the wealth we have and not block in any way our ability to increase our wealth.

Positive work and attainment of wealth support our emotional, mental, and spiritual development. But even if we maintain a healthy form of nonattachment to our material goods, we must remain aware of another product of our pursuit. Western culture is eating through the world's natural resources and the byproduct of our relentless consumerism has been an unprecedented environmental impact. In the book, Natural Capitalism,[19] the authors explain the difference between conventional capitalism and natural capitalism. Conventional capitalism propounds that in free markets, financial capital flows into those areas of service and production that most efficiently use productivity to stimulate growth, and growth and maximum profit maximize human well-being. What conventional capitalism overlooks is that the source of production is the natural capital obtained from the earth's resources. These facts are ignored on corporate balance sheets. By treating the environment as a minor factor of production and not taking into account the true costs of doing business, including consumption and the effect on the environment, conventional capitalism is unsustainable—especially as practiced in the United States and Canada—as a model for the developing nations of the world with their much larger populations.

An ecological footprint attempts to quantify the environmental capacity required to support a particular aspect of consumption, or the entire lifestyle of a population. This level of consumption can then be converted to the amount of land required to support this footprint. For everyone in the world to live at the same standard as Americans or Canadians, it's been estimated we would require the resources of two more earths. This does not factor the effect of an expanding population or an increase in worldwide standards of living, which would require several more earths to satisfy.

I have encountered a variety of responses to information such as this. First is plain denial: "That's not true," then the assertion that radical left-wing agitators who should never be trusted did the research and the results are flawed. The second response is, "Oh, my god, we're all going to die." A great deal of hand wringing, juicy epitaphs hurled at the evil-doers in government and industry who are leading us down this path to destruction, the purchase of a Prius, and a trip to the local natural foods purveyor accompany this position. The third response, often coming from those with fundamental Christian beliefs, is that this may well be true, but it is immaterial because: (1) God has given man dominion over the earth and it is His will that we fully use the earth's bounty so graciously bestowed on His children. This is usually accompanied by the unexpressed belief that the end of days is rapidly approaching so what does it matter anyway; (2) Though this may be true, we can't be sure until we have done much more research and, regardless of the final data, the scientific capabilities of man are so great that by the time we run out of anything we will have developed new technologies to take its place.

The three responses vary greatly, but they do have a common bond: total narcissism. Think of the earth as a living organism. Let's call her Gaia, who happens to be a close friend. Upon finding out that she may be unhealthy, probably because of your actions, your response is, "How does this affect me?" By far the most self-centered responses come from the smug fundamentalists who believe themselves immune to the consequences of any action because they are "saved."

One of the life's great challenges facing any individual, especially regarding money and material wealth, is developing the necessary mental and emotional faculties, and a healthy dose of compassion, not to fall victim to this pandemic of self-absorption.

Maximize Your MoneyForce: Physical Money

A healthy body is the foundation to experiencing the joy and fulfillment of money. Although we need our health for all physical experience, it is just as certain that we cannot have good emotional and mental health without a sound body. Unfortunately, in our fast-paced, work-driven society we do not often practice good health. The American corporation, though a model for productivity and profit, is a pressure cooker for those who toil for the benefit of the corporate shareholder. Many have offered emotional critiques of our corporate work ethos, decrying the immoral nature of the corporation. I would disagree. The corporation, by definition, is amoral. Immorality implies a conscious turn from moral principles, whereas amorality denotes a complete indifference to moral conduct. If the former is a sin of commission, the latter is a sin of omission.

The corporation is bound by a legal contract, a covenant if you will, between the officers and board of directors of the corporation and the shareholders. They are legally bound to promote the business activity solely for the shareholders' economic benefit. If they breech this obligation, they may be held liable for their actions. Following World War II, when corporate culture began to take on the structure we recognize today, the world economy was recovering from the devastating effect of both world wars, and we had no competition because every other competitor had blown each other to bits.

Today with a true world economy, competition is intense, and the drive for hard-earned profits has created a work culture that may easily be compared to a level of Dante's inferno. It is said that where Europeans work to live, Americans live to work. We work long hours under stressful conditions. Many people make handsome salaries and accrue comfortable lifestyles. But many Americans do not have the time to enjoy the fruits of their labors. How often do we hear of a corporate executive who, after years of struggle to reach the pinnacle of business, dies right before or after retirement?

A sad, ironic example involves McDonalds. In addition to the stress we put upon our bodies in the conditions in which we choose to work, we are a nation content to put unhealthy food in our bodies. McDonalds has been successful, but their menu has never been known as healthy. I once had a neighbor, the wife of a Japanese expatriate who, during a traditional Japanese dinner party at their home, commented there was more fat in a single chicken McNugget than she consumed in a month. Some years ago, the chairman of McDonalds died of a heart attack. Just as tragic was the news that the man's successor, an Australian who had begun his career as a line worker, had colorectal cancer. Although we can all feel for the families of the two men, it is ironic this would occur in a corporation that is an icon of a profit-driven corporate culture and an American diet overloaded with fat and fried foods.

If you want to maximize your MoneyForce, it is important to be conscious of your body and how you take care of it. Think of a car. If all you want is a beater that looks like hell and is designed to be run unto the ground, it certainly doesn't matter a bit what fuel you use or maintenance you do. But if you enjoy the ride and comfort of a luxury sedan or a high-performance sports car, it becomes essential that you use the proper fuel and observe a regular maintenance schedule.

The same is true with our bodies. If we want to benefit from the fruits of our hard-earned wealth, we must eat right and keep a sound exercise schedule. We may not be able to change the culture around us, but we can control how we live in that culture and choose to make conscious choices about the food we eat and the way we manage stress through regular exercise.

Our Money Karma

It's difficult to speak the word karma and discuss the idea with a western audience, or at least an audience immersed in the Judeo-Christian tradition, that does not teach or acknowledge its existence. Much of this comes from Hindu believers, with their misguided interpretation of karma. They treat cows as sacred, allowing them to wander the streets while they treat some people—those the caste system designates as untouchables—worse than most animals. Also, when the West began to incorporate certain ideas associated with Eastern religions, including karma and the transmigration of the soul, it was showcased amidst a mad swirl of sixties counterculture accompanied by drugs, rock music, alienation from traditional authority, women's rights, and a large dose of plain old weirdness.

That was unfortunate because the basic concept of karma transcends culture and religion. The idea "as you reap so shall you sow" is not foreign to Christians. For those with a more scientific approach, the basic tenant of karma is somewhat contained in Newton's third law of motion: "For each action there is an equal and opposite reaction."

Ralph Waldo Emerson, our native transcendental master, spoke of karma in his essay, "Compensation." Emerson understood that we pay a price to lead a spiritual life, and this price extends into the realm of our daily pursuit of commerce and possessions. Another way of looking at this is the old saying "Be careful what you wish for, you may get it." It may seem that fate, ordained by our previous actions, determines our material wealth, but this is only partly true. Good and bad money karma exist, and there is no reason why people cannot receive either or both within their lifetime. All of us can remember a rags-to-riches story and conversely a riches-to-rags story. The key is to understand there is a reason for our relationship with money, which often can be traced to actions that occurred long in the past during previous lives. We have a responsibility to apply ourselves to working out those consequences and being grateful for the blessing for past good.

Our Vows

Our subconscious and unconscious minds influence much of our ability to obtain and retain money while maintaining a healthy attitude towards our wealth. One of the best ways to reprogram our hardwiring is through conscious vows. When I began my business career, I spent a great deal of time studying the professional path of successful entrepreneurs and business people. I found one trait they all had in common was a strong positive mental and emotional attitude. They did not allow negative thoughts to cloud their vision of success. I read a great deal on this subject, including Napoleon Hill's *Think and Grow Rich*,[20] Clement Stone's and Hill's *Success Through a Positive Mental Attitude*,[21] and Dale Carnegie's *How to Win Friends and Influence People*.[22] I listened to the Nightengale-Conant tapes, which included several that used vows to alter our neurolinguistic programming.

Have you ever seen an athlete concentrating before an event? Think of the skier facing a descent down a slippery mountain at speeds of over sixty miles per hour, where the slightest misstep can cost hundredths of a second and, at worst, a life-threatening fall. The skier is absorbed in thought, moving her hands back and forth as she visualizes or imagines every move she will make as she skies the course.

By the same token, those of us who wish to break established patterns of thought and behavior that block the success we want to achieve can benefit from using this technique, which we will explore in the following exercise:

Exercise 3: Making Vows

Begin by sitting quietly and practicing the meditation technique. Before making any vows, it is important to first recite the following karmic clause and the first four vows to avoid nullifying subsequent vows:

"All of the following vows are to be done in accordance with my conscious choice, my conscious will, the will of pure God, and the highest karmic laws."

Then repeat out loud or to yourself the following vows of your choice:

1. Everything I do now, every energy I express on any level or any plane—physical, astral, mental, soul, or spiritual—will be in accordance with my conscious will, my conscious choice, the will of pure God, and the highest karmic laws.

2. Any vows I choose to make apply to the past, present, and the future.

3. Neither I, nor any part of my being, will ever go or try to go against the highest karmic laws.

4. I will never misuse vow energies for a negative purpose. I will never misuse any energies coming from any vow I have ever made or will ever make.

5. Nothing I think or say will become a vow unless I consciously choose to make it so.

6. I will never put power, energy, or force behind anything I say, feel, or think, unless I consciously choose to do so.

7. I will be able and will begin to overcome all negative experiences. I will make positive, conscious decisions and choices about what I want and need in my life.

8. I revoke any vows, anywhere, by me or for me, which are now limiting me and my ability to achieve my full potential on any level, and would or could limit me in the future.

9. I will gain control of myself in all my bodies, on all levels.

10. More money is coming to me, beginning now, in a positive way, and I will enjoy receiving it.

9
The Wheel of Life

Throughout the next week, Baraja practiced bringing different colors into his bodies and was amazed at how he could feel their powers and use them as he was developing his own renewed faculties and abilities. Yet the more he practiced and felt himself growing in spirit, the more he was troubled by a great paradox that had bothered him all his adult life. At the next lesson he asked the Master, "It seems to me that often the basest people are the most rich and powerful. How can that be?"

Amatamaji thought for a moment, her face inscrutable, and then replied, "Each of us, with our special characteristics, is born into a family and an environ-ment that seems either helpful or inimical to our progress. In reality, all circum-stances are opportunities, for they are the natural results of our past way of life and the stepping-stones of our future growth. Progress is easier to achieve if we view our destiny as the product of our own efforts, rather than something that is imposed upon us. Each day we weave the threads of our own futures. We are all born at the specific time we have merited, into conditions we have earned, and opportunities that are suitable to the next stage of development for which we are ready. Each person finds himself within those circumstances he has earned. If he is dissatisfied with his present condition, then it is up to him to create within himself those causes that will result in effects he will find more to his satisfaction.

"Before you, a soul personality, were ever attracted or assigned to a definite physical body, you had the privilege of reviewing several possibilities that could be offered in your next life, You were shown certain opportunities that would enable you to learn, work out your past karma, expand your consciousness, and move ever closer to the complete and full expression of that particular God-quality your soul selected prior to your first incarnation in a physical form.

"It is not unusual for the more advanced soul to attempt to select the most difficult path, rather than the easiest of those offered him, because his primary objective is to regain as quickly as possible that state of balance that will enable him to be free. This is not ordinarily permitted, because it is possible the load could be too great a burden for his physical-emotional-mental nature. If the load proved too heavy, the result would be a breakdown. As a consequence, the soul is generally guided to select the path that will enable him to grow as much as possible without jeopardizing his highest welfare in the process.

"Not every soul personality is this dedicated to growth. Only a few attempt to select the most difficult path. The majority of souls seek to reincarnate as soon as possible without being concerned about growth and development. These goals and ideals hold less appeal to them than the desire to be reborn to once again experience the emotions that accompany life in the physical. There are some souls who do not wish to reincarnate, and who try to remain overlong in the psychic realm. For their own good, they are eventually forced to re-enter the physical realm, but they no longer have any voice in the selection of time, place, or family environment.

"Your hearing my words indicates that most of you have reached the point in your spiritual development where you have selected the body you inhabit, the opportunities that have been presented to you, and the life you are now leading. Your life and the opportunities within it have probably been altered at least once since your birth, for this is true of almost everyone who is interested in learning about self-development. Dedication to the idea of self-development and the desire to expand your consciousness creates changes in your life and offers you numerous opportunities for diminishing your negative karma. These opportunities will eventually give you a greater understanding of life and its creator.

"The ensuing lifetime offers the opportunity to balance the debts incurred in your previous lives and permits others to repay you for the help you gave them. We were each given certain energies, or raw material, with which to achieve this objective, on the condition that we return them in as pure a state as they were when we received them. Today we are beginning to correct our karmic mistakes by restoring these energies to the original state we changed by misusing them. With each breath, we draw energies into our bodies and our auras. These fresh, clean, pure, unsullied energies were originally given to us with the understanding we use them in an unselfish and impersonal manner. If we use the energies in this way, they remain pure. If not, they become impure.

"Karma is neither fate nor predestination. The application of this natural law does away with any possibility of such a thing as luck, either good or bad. Behind every piece of good fortune lie the causes that the individual has either consciously or unconsciously precipitated, perhaps recently or in a previous life. Behind every bit of bad fortune lies the energy likewise generated by the person himself. Although it is true your accumulated karma either helps or hinders your progress, you are still free to choose within the limits you have made for yourself. By successive choices and effort, or by a lack of effort, you determine the orbit of your freedom. Fatalism or predestination implies the individual is so bound by circumstances or by some outside power that no effort of his own can free him. Under the operation of karmic law, he who generates the causes or forces can modify or neutralize them. Consequently, now you possess the power to modify your past karma and, as a result, improve your future."

"In my daily life, how can I be aware of my actions, especially as they affect my material well-being?" Baraja asked.

"The process of evolution gradually forces us to learn, unlearn, and relearn. When circumstances are altered for one reason or another, we are frequently faced with the choice of experiencing the change, loss, or gain in a positive, neutral, or negative way. Our reaction determines the karma created, and offers us, and others, the opportunity to evolve, remain static, or regress. The karma we accumulate determines the frequency and extensiveness of the tests we encounter. They often involve various aspects of life, but can remain concentrated in one particular area. In passing these tests, we reap the positive benefits of developing our potential and furthering our evolution. Should we fail them, we will continue to be confronted with these or similar experiences until we master them.

"When we decide to improve ourselves, we set into motion a purification process that involves our deleting the majority of negative aspects from our consciousness. This process generally occurs on all levels. Physical or emotional problems, or both, conflicting inner and outer attitudes, financial difficulties, and the uprooting of many cherished beliefs are a few of the confrontations that can happen independently or as part of a series of occurrences in our lives. New growth seldom comes without giving up or changing our former approach to life. This frequently encompasses a number of challenges and hardships that require patience and perseverance to overcome. It is encouraging to remember that as the beautiful lotus blooms atop the water with its roots deeply embedded in mud, so, too, can we ultimately surmount our frustrations and blossom amidst the many challenges encountered along truth's path.

"Your attitude and the way you feel towards life are important. You can gain a great deal of satisfaction if you become involved—in your daily toil, for instance—to the extent you can truly enjoy it. With this positive state of mind, you can use your potential to the best of your ability to accomplish your tasks. On the other hand, if you become too involved, you can allow your work to become the all-consuming motivation in your life. Should this happen, your work could become your life's purpose, an end in itself instead of a means to an end—that of providing for yourself and possibly others. Many are unable to keep work in its proper perspective, time, and place. If you become excessively attached to your work, you may find yourself anxious and frustrated by constantly wondering whether you will achieve that which you set out to do. A more moderate attitude towards life can stimulate accomplishment of your desired results without the impatience and lack of peace that a less well-balanced approach generates.

"Should a task be difficult, recognize that fact, then visualize and imagine yourself accomplishing it more efficiently. This will frequently require a change of attitude, but one that will result in the availability of more time, energy, and the creative ability to achieve what you desire. Enter into your work wholeheartedly. When it is completed—for the hour, the day, or even that particular task—release it and go on to your next task. The attitude of mastering your work rather than allowing it to become your master is something to strive for if you wish to achieve greater fulfillment in life."

"Why do I feel I can't achieve the success I strive for in my life?" Baraja interjected. "It seems like I am always putting up barriers for myself or others place barriers in front of me."

"Since the beginning of time," the patient Master answered, "we have made and created vows for ourselves through our own thoughts and words, and others have made vows for us through their thoughts and words. It is likely we have made vows unconsciously for ourselves or others have made vows for us that have had a positive, helpful influence upon us. It is also likely we have unconsciously made harmful or detrimental vows for ourselves or others, because those vows put blocks in our path that are now hindering us from gaining mastery and enlightenment.

"Once we determine what the blocks are, we can then begin to remove them and clear them away. The words we hear and speak, the way we feel, and the things we do all have the potential to become a vital force in our lives. The subconscious is the part of our mind programmed during this lifetime. The unconscious is that part in which we accumulated programming from previous lifetimes. For example, if we had over 900,000 previous lifetimes, can you imagine the programming we could have, positive or negative, and the vows we may have made such as 'I will love you forever,' or 'It is such a struggle to realize my wishes?' Subconscious programming could take place consciously or unconsciously, but even when our subconscious programming takes place unconsciously, it still has a profound effect and influence on our lives."

Amatamaji looked at her students and waited in silence for the question she knew would come. Baraja did not disappoint. "You speak of past lives and the reincarnation cycle. How can something I did in another life, of which I have no conscious memory, control my life today?"

"When one is in the reincarnation cycle, he is involuting. That means he is going down into denser matter to reach the bottom of the low physical plane before evolving, or coming back up, through all the planes to complete the reunification with God. During evolution, our lower bodies, the physical, astral, and mental, work to gain mastery of the lower planes. When we have achieved this, there is no longer a need to return to the earth or to the physical plane. It is at this time that the soul begins its journey in the higher planes, known as the spiritual planes. Once the soul begins its spiritual journey, we can master the high planes much more quickly while living in a physical body. When the time comes for the soul to begin its journey in the higher planes, its negative karma becomes balanced.

"Soon after the soul gains entrance into the soul planes and is totally activated, the soul has the choice for future lifetimes to remain in the soul planes or return to the lower planes to grow and evolve. When someone is out of the reincarnation cycle, he has the choice to return to Earth or to any lower planets, at any time he chooses. The soul, with balanced negative karma, can be assured to some degree that few, if any, attachments strong enough to force its return to Earth exist. If there were any karma to force the soul to return to Earth or to the lower planets to repay a debt, it would be offset by all the positive karma the soul had accumulated. The accumulated positive karma would continue to accrue.

"The soul begins to learn, after dwelling in the higher planes, that the physical presents opportunities for much faster growth than working in the spiritual planes. The lower planes offer the most opportunity to grow and evolve. The soul might choose, then, to return to the physical or go instead to an astral or a mental planet.

"There are two things you should be aware of by now. First, whether we like it or not, we are all programmed individuals. Second, a lot of that programming is a result of statements, affirmations, or vows we made in either this life or a past life. We make vows by what we say and think, on every level of our being.

"We can change the negative influences in our lives, and we can also strive to strengthen the positive influences. You must choose what you want and do not want. Monitor your thoughts and take the steps to see what influences are in your life. Following that, set up positive energies to attract what you positively will, desire, and think about. It's the greatest of all opportunities for your spiritual growth. Making vows helps. If we are constantly muddled with programmed thoughts, feelings, and actions from the past, it's difficult to see from a clear perspective. When you are up to your knees in mud, it's hard to see dry land. We have to start by clearing a little path to see where the dry land is, where we will find clarity."

10
Astral Money, Blue

"It is that whole system of appetites and values with its deification of snatching to hoard and hoarding to snatch, which now, in the hour of its triumph, while the plaudits of the crowd still ring in the ears of the gladiators and the laurels are still unfaded on their brows, seems sometimes to leave a taste of ashes on the lips of a civilization which has brought to the conquest of its material environment resources unknown in earlier ages, but which has not yet learned to master itself."
—R. H. Tawney[23]

Introduction

Blue is the color of peace and faith. It is often said that Americans are obsessed with material possessions. Although it is certainly true that developed western societies operate on a consumer-based economy, and we are indoctrinated since birth to consume, it is not the physical possession with which we are obsessed. We exist in the physical plane, but we spend a good part of our conscious hours in the astral—the emotional—plane, and our desire for material possessions is primarily emotional. In this chapter we will explore how to recognize and harness our emotions to further the development of our MoneyForce.

How We Relate to Astral Money

In a PBS Frontline documentary, "The Persuaders," which covered the effect of advertising on our lives, a market researcher claimed that our emotions spur eighty percent of our actions. This man believed the words used to describe things trigger emotional reactions that determine how we respond to a situation. The Republican Party often used this researcher to help candidates find the most emotionally potent words to use when speaking to the electorate. It was his suggestion to change the name of the estate tax—the tax charged to a decedent's property, or estate.

The researcher discovered, using focus groups, that the term "estate tax" had little effect upon the study group, whereas the term "death tax" elicited a strong response. Many of us understand the word estate, but it has little practical meaning in our lives. We have a hard enough time living from one paycheck to another, and the prospect of building an "estate" seems highly unlikely. Yet death is a fact of life with which we are all painfully aware on a daily basis. Shifting the focus from the source of taxation, the estate, to the event of the taxation, death, completely changes and charges the emotional content of the issue. Think of the difference in feeling when the word "income tax" is changed to "work tax." We are more detached from the word "income" than from the word "work." Or try "paycheck tax." When a word is linked to deep emotional feelings, it is much more powerful.

Politicians use these emotional triggers in both directions. Where using death tax rather than estate tax brings out a strong emotional response against taxing our hard-earned assets at death, using the term "global climate change" rather than "global warming" tends to lessen the emotional impact of that issue. The weather is unpredictable and changes everyday. Why get upset about normal changing weather? This presents a different emotional response than that implicated by "global warming," with its image of melting polar caps, rising sea levels, and the cataclysmic results these changes could bring.

Linguistics professor George Lakoff has studied language use, especially metaphor, in how our brains frame an issue. Professor Lakoff studied the work of Frank Luntz, a Republican pollster who helped Newt Gingrich develop the Contract with America, and then formulated his political theories on the results. Politicians can frame an issue to their design by using language that touches people on a subconscious level. For example, instead of saying, "drilling for oil," they might say "exploring for energy." Rather than criticize "government," which provides necessary services, they would substitute "Washington," which conjures a cabal of immoral politicians.

In his article, "The Framing Wars," published in *The New York Times Magazine* of July 17, 2005, Matt Bai explores the use of language in the political arena. Bai says that Democrats have made the mistake of thinking people are rational and make decisions solely on facts. It has been shown that our responses are often not logical and come from emotional responses to frames embedded in our subconscious. These frames are more powerful than any facts that may be presented to us and, when the facts don't fit the frame, we simply reject the facts. During the Watergate investigation, I heard on the Today show one of President Richard Nixon's ardent supporters, when presented with overwhelming evidence of the president's guilt, responded, "Don't confuse me with the facts." During the 2016 Republican primary and the General Election the candidate Donald Trump broke every convention of moral discourse and public decorum in his attempt to appeal to the raw emotions of his followers, mostly in a very base manner. Against every prediction Trump became President although without winning a majority of the popular vote.

With respect to money, it is our emotions, often buried in our subconscious, that drive our relationship with the acquisition of wealth and what we do with the wealth we possess. My professional career involved advising people on how to plan for their financial success. After observing hundreds of individuals, I would say their emotions have by far the greatest effect on their behavior when money is concerned. Most financial planners, if they are to have any success, learn early that their primary job in dealing with clients is managing the client's expectations and emotions.

The financial planning process begins for most people in their late thirties. They have established their careers and have increasing family responsibilities. They are beginning to think beyond their own narcissistic, adolescent desires and recognize the need to plan for the future. All physical resources are, by definition, finite. Financial planning requires discipline. Most financial plans require a balance between future goals and immediate gratification.

For example, a regular savings program is often the only way to build sufficient resources to meet the rapidly growing costs of higher education for a child. Yet the money dedicated to that need is money not available for current consumption. This will naturally lead to an emotional dilemma. We love our children and want the best for their future security, but we also have our own desires for comfort, status, and security. We often don't understand these desires well because they come from deep emotional undercurrents in our unconscious mind. Our emotional responses are usually not derived from a rational analysis. How often do you experience or hear of a shopping spree triggered in response to an emotional crisis? Many people reward themselves with food to satiate deep emotional insecurity. Shopping fulfills the same craving. The need is not met in either case. The individual is treating the symptom, not the cause. The result in the first case is unwanted pounds and, in the second, the accumulation of unnecessary stuff that is soon forgotten and pushed to the back of a cluttered closet.

The choice often comes to setting priorities. When we set up a college fund, for example, is our love for our children and the satisfaction we gain from accepting our responsibilities greater than the gratification we get from spending the money on ourselves? Fortunately, as most people mature and grow, that choice becomes easier.

Another example that does not bring the emotional aspect of our children's welfare into play is retirement. Here our emotions are soundly centered on one key point: am I willing to defer current pleasure—receiving and spending money now—for the sense of security and attainment of the desired lifestyle I want in retirement? This decision is usually deferred as our career develops, our family's needs increase, and our sense of mortality takes shape. For most, this doesn't happen until the mid to late forties when the bloom is off the rose of our youthful hopes and dreams, years of toil begin to have an effect, and the prospect of not only retiring but taking early retirement becomes the object of dreams, day and night.

In this instance, the emotional quandary is often presented in the cost of deferring current consumption—by this time the dream of retirement is much stronger than the prospect of another unwanted possession—and in the risk decisions that must be made when determining how to invest the retirement savings. It is this decision that triggers the two most common emotions anyone ever faces when relating to money: greed and fear.

Retirement planning is a good example of how emotions affect behavior. Retirement planning variables are: when to retire, living expenses in retirement, the length of retirement, the amount required to fund the retirement needs, and the rate of return on savings before and during retirement. We can easily see the decisions that must be made. Defer retirement and the amount a retiree will spend is reduced, but less money will need to be saved to meet those goals. If the retirement date is earlier without changing the amount of funding, it will require a higher rate of return to maintain the target retirement lifestyle

Although there are several variations of the types of decisions that can be made with the different variables, the main issue always comes down to the question of, how much risk am I willing to take with my retirement savings? This is because the amount of retirement funding is generally going to remain somewhat constant based upon limits on retirement plan contributions and the financial limits of the individual. Although people can modify expenses in retirement, few wish to live out their golden years in a lifestyle significantly below that which they worked so hard to achieve. Finally, the date of retirement is often determined by age and cannot be easily altered.

Investment return is one variable the individual cannot control and is, therefore, the most vulnerable to emotional factors. One client I worked with, an executive with a large insurance company, was forced into early retirement at fifty-seven. He was a high-level executive earning a good salary, which he and his wife had no trouble spending every year. He had no investing experience because his entire retirement savings came from his company pension, which he decided to roll over into an IRA, and the company savings plan that had been invested in large part in company stock.

With a luxurious lifestyle, a sudden transition to retirement, no more pay-check, no background in investing, and the responsibility for managing his own financial future, he wisely decided to consult with a financial planner. In reviewing his options, we discussed the choices he needed to make regarding how the retirement assets would be invested to meet his current and future income needs, which would be affected by inflation.

The client expressed great comfort with his choice of investments that historically provided greater total return and would allow him to maintain his accustomed lifestyle. We discussed the fact that, although these investments had indeed provided a greater return in the past, they had done so with much greater volatility and higher risk than other investments. I explained his choice was to accept the risk of some loss of principal during short-term down markets to achieve the greater, long-term return expected. We discussed the only way to achieve this, other than being able to predict the future and never be invested when the market was going down, was to have the emotional fortitude to ride out the temporary losses when they occurred.

The client assured me this would be no problem. Unfortunately, his resolve was soon put to the test with sad results. Several months after investing his retirement savings in a portfolio designed to increase over time but with a greater risk of loss in the short term, the stock market suffered a major correction and the client's funds went down in value.

His response was immediate and visceral. The emotional reality of seeing losses in his investments was devastating, even though we had discussed the risks and they were documented in an agreement he signed. He immediately closed his accounts and invested the entire amount of this savings in the safest investments he could find. It didn't matter to him that the return on these safe investments could not meet even his current income needs, let alone provide for his ever-inflating expenses in the future. He was blinded by his fear and instinctually doing what he needed to remove the emotion, much in the same way people pull their hands from fire to avoid getting burned.

Sadly for this man, the market soon corrected and the investments he held originally regained their value and went on during the subsequent years to achieve returns far above what we originally expected. To compound the error of his emotional response, the safe investments he bought during the stock market crash did not prove as safe as he thought. Although they did provide a stream of income in the form of regular interest payments, they were vulnerable to the effects of rising interest rates. During the subsequent bull market, while stock prices soared, interest rates went up as well and the value of his retirement savings went even lower.

I tell this story with a sense of regret because I continue to feel responsible for this outcome. Legally and professionally I did everything right, but my failure was in accepting at face value what I was told, without fully exploring the emotional undercurrents which, though carefully disguised, lurked just below the surface. I learned a valuable lesson for me and my succeeding clients: when it comes to money, what people think is much less important than what they feel and, even more so, what people think they know is determined by what they feel as they think. This example shows how fear can distort judgment and lead to emotional reactions that are not beneficial to your financial well-being.

The second emotional determinate is greed. Fear and greed are often mutually dependant. Many people make the mistake of investing during periods of economic prosperity when they have the surplus income to invest, and rising stock markets, supported by success stories in the press, lead to increased demand, which naturally increases stock prices. When the economy weakens, as it inevitably does during natural business cycles, demand for stocks weakens and, as prices go down, investors who bought at the top quickly lose their confidence and sell at a loss, especially when the press feeds their fear with horror stories of impending doom. These normal bull and bear market cycles occasionally experience an extraordinary event known as a market bubble, when prices in certain markets explode to stratospheric levels, only to crash with equally dramatic results.

An example of this was in 1998 and 1999 when the prices of technology stocks in general, and Internet and telecommunications stocks specifically, exploded in a classic bubble. In early 2000 I captured the frenzy of the period in an article I wrote for my client newsletter: "During a meeting, a client had expressed dissatisfaction with their investment return for the year. I was somewhat surprised because the return was over twenty-five percent and was over eighty percent in excess of the weighted market index benchmark. It seems in this investment environment it is not sufficient for investors to be happy. They must be ecstatic. Using a disciplined process of diversification can be challenging. Asset allocation is founded on the premise that while it is extremely difficult to predict future security prices and time the market effectively, it is possible to manage the risk of investment through a prudent investment process. This method is based upon the assumption that investors are risk-adverse. The system will be challenged during periods of risk oblivion such as the one we were experiencing.'

'At this time when I met with clients and pointed out that their under-performing assets for 1999 significantly outperformed their markets and peers, they often looked at me as if I were from another planet. In a diversified asset allocation, we assume that different assets will perform independently of one another. That is how we manage investment risk. In addition, it is likely that assets performing poorly during one period will often rebound strongly. It is the simple old adage, "buy low and sell high." Unfortunately, during periods of "irrational exuberance", investors are far more inclined to ignore the sale and pay ever-higher prices for already overpriced securities.'

'The irrationality and absurdity of the market psychology of that time is exemplified by a phone call I had with a young executive of a start-up dot .com company that was attempting to raise money. When I said there were no financial statements in the offering memorandum, he replied, "Internet stocks don't have financials." He then commenced on a half hour diatribe of technical doublespeak attempting to justify why traditional financial methodology (like making a profit) had no bearing in this market. When I asked him how many business cycles he had experienced in his career he replied, "Two. Reality and the Internet.'

'I suppose this meant that because he had never experienced a recession during the five years since he left school and had been immersed in the Internet during that time he was exempt from the traditional rules of economic order under which the rest of we mere mortals toil. Well, he may be right. Then again don't bet the family farm. Ever hear the saying "Famous last words?"

The clients referenced in my newsletter where two well-educated professionals who allowed themselves to get caught up in irrational mania. I remember well the review meeting we had in January 2000. I was looking forward to it because the performance of the client's well-diversified portfolio, although not achieving the triple-digit returns provided by Internet and telecommunication stocks, had returned close to twenty-eight percent, and, more importantly, had outperformed the market benchmark (a comparison standard for performance comprised of representative index funds allocated in the same manner as the client's portfolio) by over seventy percent. I was especially proud of this because the large concentration of return in a small number of stocks in some market indices made it difficult for most money managers to outperform their benchmark targets in 1999.

The client began the meeting with the words, "We are very disappointed."

When I picked my jaw off the table and asked why, they responded, "There was a negative return in our real estate mutual fund." This was true and, although I pointed out that all real estate performed poorly in 1998 and 1999 and this fund did much better than most, they looked at me as if I had lost all contact with reality.

The client insisted that the money allocated to the poorly performing real estate investments be placed in the highest performing technology stocks. When I refused this request as imprudent and not in their best interest, I was promptly fired. I assume they were able to find another advisor more than willing to feed their greed. Unfortunately, this occurred exactly at the top of the technology bubble and prices on those overpriced securities fell over the next three years as much as ninety percent. At the same time, real estate experienced a boom, in large part due to lower interest rates, and led most sectors of the market in performance.

These examples provide anecdotal evidence of the effect emotion can have on our attitude and decisions about money. They reinforce the importance of recognizing our emotions regarding money and how we relate to it. There has been much research into the different ways people relate to money from a psychological, or emotional, perspective. Different typologies have been developed to attempt to categorize different money personalities. Sociologist, criminologist, and psychotherapist Lewis Yablonsky in his book, *The Emotional Meaning of Money*[24] identifies five money styles:

1. Contented: Not driven towards specific goals but are content with their given level of wealth.

2. Logical Achievers: Have specific goals they wish to attain and, once achieved, are content.

3. Emotionally Unaffected Strivers: Driven by goals and achievement but do not let either the process or the success or failure of their effort affect their personal or emotional life.

4. Emotionally Affected Strivers: Allow the ups and downs of the struggle to attain financial goals to become a source of pain and suffering.

5. Insatiables: Pursue money, power, and prestige to fill an inner psyche void that can never be satisfied.

In her book, *Your Money Personality*,[25] Los Angeles psychologist Kathleen Gurney identifies nine distinct money personalities:

> Entrepreneurs
> Hunters
> High Rollers
> Safety Players
> Achievers
> Perfectionists
> Money Masters
> Producers
> Optimists

Although these typologies are useful in identifying distinct behavioral tendencies, they often have limited use for individuals who wish to modify the way they relate to money. Concerned individuals wishing to understand and control a certain behavior, especially if it has pathological results, are not the primary users of these typologies. Financial service providers use this information to better understand the behavior of different money profiles and increase their chances of attracting new business or improve their ability to communicate with existing clients.

For you to achieve your MoneyForce it is vitally important that you understand the impact of your emotions on the decisions you make, the source of those emotions, and how to achieve a balance in your emotional life. Tim Kasser, a psychology professor at Knox College, conducted a study on the relationship between emotional well-being and the pursuit of materialistic values. As people put more energy into obtaining material goods, they put less emphasis on developing and maintaining close personal connections within their community of family and friends. As this developed, there was an increased sense of conflict and alienation.

Kasser identified three ways in which materialistic values detract from our emotional well- being:

1. They support a sense of insecurity.
2. They lead to an endless pursuit of proving our competence.
3. They block our relationships.

He also believes these lead to less freedom and a need for authenticity and autonomy. The more we pursue material values, the less focused we are on our individual sense of purpose and personal identity. Our pursuit of wealth controls us and we lose our identity, which is necessary for a strong sense of self to enjoy the fruits of our efforts. When this happens, our material values no longer support and serve our interpersonal values and we feel bound to our material pursuit.

Money and Religion

Religion is certainly an emotional topic. We mentioned briefly Jesus' teachings relative to physical wealth. It may be useful now to take a look at the effect religion has on our emotional attitudes towards money. Religion and money have dominated my academic and professional life. I have a master's degree in religious studies and had a thirty-year career as a financial advisor. In retirement I have become an historian having authored The Great American Turquoise Rush, 1890-1910.

We will focus our attention on Christianity because it is the largest religion in the United States and the developed western nations. The United States was founded on the principal of personal freedom: freedom of religious practice and freedom of personal economic development central to the elusive pursuit of happiness. The pilgrims were Calvinists who followed a severe Protestant doctrine, which fostered the belief that an individual's eternal salvation was predestined and no amount of good works in life would alter this inexorable path. Much has been made of the effect of this form of Calvinist Protestant doctrine on Americans' work attitude, mainly by sociologist Max Weber.

Weber uses Ben Franklin as a representative of the uniquely American attitudes about work, money, and religion. We are all well aware of the aphorisms found in _Poor Richard's Almanac_ such as "Early to bed, early to rise makes a man healthy, wealthy, and wise," and "Remember that time is money."

We would think a religious doctrine promoting preordained salvation would lead to an ambivalent life at best or a profligate life at worst. In practice, the Puritans were extreme in their pursuit of worldly possessions and position. It was as if to justify inclusion in the ranks of the elect, it was necessary to manifest extreme good works as evidence of chosen status. Weber commented that the anxiety produced by the dilemma of not knowing whether one was saved had the opposite effect of its intent. Whereas the doctrine believed that faith alone, not works, was required for salvation, to demonstrate one's status as the elect, intense worldly effort and success were desirable, which means God helps those who help themselves.

This position can lead to an ever-increasing effort to climb the economic prosperity ladder and demonstrate our elected status. The belief, essentially an illogical misrepresentation of a religious-philosophical tenant of a sect within a sect of Christianity, is sometimes grafted to capitalism in an attempt to blend the economic system with religious practice. Weber denies this and states it is not capitalism's intent to follow unlimited greed and acquire the greatest amount of money, but that "capitalism is identical with the pursuit of ... profit, by means of continuous, capitalistic enterprise."

It would seem it is not the system of capitalism that creates the propensity for greedy pursuit of material well-being—to the exclusion of developing all else—but rather the attitudes and beliefs society brings to the system. By this logic, the system would just as easily support an economy based upon low growth and sustainable resource. Economist Maynard Keynes noted capitalism is irreligious in that it is not concerned with issues of the public spirit. Put another way, capitalism is amoral not immoral. Corporate boards of directors are legally bound to pursue those actions that will most benefit the shareholders of the company, regardless of the consequences of those actions on society.

All spiritual traditions hold that the essence of being is recognizing an inner world and the higher force guiding that being. All social institutions have developed with the goal of maintaining a close connection with that inner world while pursuing the daily struggle for survival in the outer world. Over time the connection between the inner and outer world has been forgotten and the outer world has come to dominate our sense of reality. The outer world existed at one time only for us to experience our inner reality more fully. Now the outer world appears to be our sole level of existence. Although we may hold on to some theoretical belief in the inner world through our religious doctrines, in practice we value the external world much more.

Maximize Your MoneyForce: Astral Money

It is one thing to understand and desire the "realm between the two worlds," yet it is quite another thing to experience it. One of the difficulties with most religions is that the effort required to fulfill the promise is so great most believers settle for fervent belief and strict adherence to a set of rules they feel meet the religion's requirements.

Though the goal is daunting, the practice is remarkably easy and quite natural if we approach it with the right attitude and expectation. Most religious devotees expect transcendence immediately, and this is contrary to all natural laws. If you want to run a marathon, you don't show up at the race with no preparation. You run a mile, then two, for several weeks. At first the sore muscles may make it difficult to get out there every day, but if you persevere and keep to a regular schedule, soon you will run five miles with little difficulty. Over time, what once seemed impossible will be attainable because you have been focused and diligent in your practice and your body has developed to the point where you can do a twenty-six-mile run.

It is the same with any spiritual practice. Don't look to the finish line. Keep your focus on the immediate task at hand and be regular in your practice. It is quite amazing how consistent most religions are in their basic practice, regardless of the differences in their dogma.

I remember a professional conference I once attended where the keynote speaker was Sir John Templeton, the famous investor and former head of the Templeton Funds. The attendees, professional financial advisors, anxiously waited for the moment of transcendence when Sir John would unveil the innermost secrets necessary for investment management success. After a few brief, perfunctory statements about the economy and current market conditions, Sir John, also the creator of the Templeton Award for Religion, told the audience that the basis for his economic success was never to go into debt and to tithe—give one-tenth of his income—to his chosen religion. With that he left the stage to a subdued and mostly disappointed audience. Great, if I want to be like Sir John, I need to tithe and not buy anything on credit. His simple admonition contains a great pearl of truth: every religious practice begins with giving.

Exercise 4: Spring Cleaning

1. Take an inventory of all of your possessions: clothes, shoes, coats, tools, toys, furniture, garden equipment, kitchen pots, plates, and appliances.

2. Give away twenty to thirty percent to the charity of your choice. If you have ten shirts, give away the two or three you never wear and don't like anyway.

3. Give yourself something special. Don't replace all the stuff you have just freed yourself from. Rather, find something special you will value and use. Don't be cheap. Buy something of exceptional quality, even if it is quite expensive, that will last and give pleasure and utility for a minimum of ten years.

4. Do this exercise every year until you reach the point where everything you own is special to you, is designed to last, and provides for your physical needs without the need for redundant clutter.

Take the time and effort to undertake this life cleaning. You will feel terrific after some initial misgivings and inner arguments about how essential something you haven't seen or used for the past five years is, and your home will be seem like a new place.

As you perform this annual ritual, you will find it easier to say no to those who would manipulate your emotions and weaknesses to push you onto the endless treadmill of consumerism. Say no to consumerism, say yes to saving:

Save for your body by taking control of the way you look and feel. Choose to eat right and do not be coerced by the dictates of a consumer-based economy that could care less about your well-being.

Save for the future by setting aside ten percent of what you earn.

Save for yourself by choosing to live with a purpose to balance your inner and outer worlds, recognizing true wealth exists in the realm between the two. Do this by taking the time to maintain a regular exercise program and follow a healthy diet. Do this for your spirit through a regular practice of prayer, meditation, or inner concentration and reflection.

As you practice these simple steps, you will find yourself saying yes to giving—giving to your body so you may live a full and healthy life and giving to yourself as you experience the joy that comes from following your true calling. Unite this in body and soul by giving ten percent of your earnings to your church or the charities you value. The other giving is what you pay to society in the form of taxes for the commonwealth, the shared needs we face as a nation. This leaves sixty to sixty-five percent of your earnings for personal consumption. This may sound overly simplistic, like Sir John's suggestion, but it is true. It is universal to all religions and it works.

11
Conscious Development

At his next lesson, Baraja began with a question he had been thinking about for some time. "When I look into the world, I see such a gap between the rich and the poor. It seems that everyone is obsessed with having riches, obtaining riches, or the lack of riches. Why are we all so preoccupied with accumulating wealth?"

"Whatever you imagine and desire takes place on the astral or emotional plane," Amatamaji replied. "What you think about takes place on the mental plane. Your physical activity takes place on the physical plane. Cosmic energy generates each type of activity, whether physical, astral or mental, but its own particular sound, rhythm, tone, vibration, and color differentiate it. Atoms and molecules that exist on the desire or astral level comprise what is called astral fluid. Astral energy is called psychic energy. Every time you desire or imagine something, you create a form or element on the astral plane that is empowered by a tremendous amount of psychic energy. Your emotions may be either positive or negative. When you create a positive form on the astral plane, you release positive energy as a real force behind it. When you create a negative form, negative energy is released behind it.

"When you become aware of adverse or detrimental circumstances in your life that you would like to change, you can immediately begin to create a positive picture of them in your imagination. Remember, you reap what you sow. Will it be positive or negative? Psychic energy follows each image you create. You will need to generate a strong, positive desire, feeling, or emotion to empower the image you want to manifest. You can then use this powerful force to replace the images that no longer satisfy you.

"Consider what happens when many people have the same or similar emotions or desires. How many people worry about or are afraid of the following: a dread disease; being robbed or raped; natural calamities such as drought, flood, or fire?

"What are your fears? What makes you angry? What do others do that makes you angry, resentful, or jealous? Are you responding to your thoughts or are you tuning in to what someone else is thinking or feeling? Are you tuning to mass consciousness, accepting and absorbing those thoughts and energies as your own?

"Mass consciousness is a combination of energy, power, force, and strength. When a group has like-minded negative thoughts or common fears, the energies combine to create a powerful energy form with negative power, force, and strength. It is easy to be pulled into such a form. Once that happens, what you think at that same level, whatever fears you have, will begin to work to satisfy your thoughts and desires. You will, therefore, want to avoid being pulled down into mass consciousness. One way to do this is to imagine and visualize that you are floating above the mass. Whenever you encounter negative energy and feel yourself being pulled down, imagine and visualize yourself floating up. You can't be negatively affected when you are higher in consciousness than the masses.

"It is up to you to create the most positive atmosphere you can for your life and your loved ones. It is up to you to detach yourself from negative situations and from those who might be pulled to you by negative ties and circumstances from the past. Listen. Monitor yourself to be aware of self-sabotage. Are you a victim of control from someone else's projections? Is there programming within your early life that is now influencing you to act or feel in a certain way that is not helpful or supportive of your aspirations? Watch your thoughts. Stop limiting yourself and judging yourself and others. Stop condemning others. Every time you say something limiting or you judge someone, the color green goes out of your aura. Pink enters your aura every time you say something kind and loving to someone.

"All forms of life are in a continual process of change. The universe changes. People change physically, emotionally, mentally, and spiritually throughout their lives. Handling changes in a positive manner is one of the most difficult things for individuals to learn to do. Sometimes you can control your changes, sometimes you cannot. You may be separated from loved ones. The quantity, severity, and frequency of changes determine the degree of tension, anxiety, and nervousness you experience. The pace and frequency of changes within society create anxiety for many people. It is not only the negative changes that cause this. Positive changes such as marriage, moving, and working at something you enjoy can also make you tense or anxious.

"Many individuals resist change, and this can lead to physical ailments. Change can turn into a negative experience when we become stagnant in our thinking. You need to deal with all change in a flexible, fluid manner. When you learn something new, you often feel apprehensive. But after you master the lesson and become proficient at it, you can feel proud of yourself and your accomplishments and go on to learn something else.

"Changing does not always come naturally. You may resist change because it was emotionally painful in the past, but the more you use and develop your will faculty, the stronger it will become and the easier it will be to have particular dreams and goals come true.

"A positive sign of emotional and mental health is learning to deal successfully with ambiguity and life changes. It is important to be open to new ideas and thoughts. Being open means you do not reject new ideas or attitudes just because you currently do not believe in them. Being open means you allow other people to have values and ideas that are different from yours, and you accept their differences without the need to diminish their respect and worth.

"Each time you change, you give up something and replace it with something better. The result is you move to a higher level of conscious awareness. You may be working, for example, to give up an angry, hot temper for a more understanding, accepting nature. As you give up old attitudes, habits, and beliefs, you can replace them with attitudes and beliefs that will make you a happier, more fulfilled, and confident person."

"How does our astral body, our emotional self, affect our relationship with our material wealth?" Baraja asked.

"Although the thought process is a function of the mental plane, and emotions, feelings, and desires originate on the astral plane, energies from the two planes work in conjunction with each other. Emotional and desire energy, for instance, frequently empower feeling and thought. The greater the intensity of psychic energy you add to feeling and thought, the stronger they become and the more rapidly you can expect them to manifest. They tend to manifest in direct proportion to the amount of energy you put behind them. By carefully conserving and utilizing your psychic energy, you can direct it towards one or two of the endeavors you feel you would most like to accomplish at this time. When you have achieved these, direct your psychic energy towards successfully completing one or two more endeavors. You will be far more effective in achieving the end results you desire if you limit the number you work with at any one time. In this way you will avoid splitting your energies. If you were to do so, you would not be able to effectively achieve what you set out to accomplish.

"It is not only important to know how to add psychic energy to empower your emotions, feelings, and desires, but also important to learn to work with and diminish the negative energy contained in the emotional expressions you feel but do not want to manifest. Once you cause the positive energy within a situation to become more powerful than the negative, you replace disharmonious energies with harmonious ones. By doing this, you will help restore peace and harmony to a situation that formerly contained disharmonious energies."

"It sounds like you are saying that to direct positive psychic energy towards our desire to accumulate material wealth we must remove our negative emotions," Baraja interjected.

"Yes," Amatamaji replied. "It is important to mention here that part of the responsibility involved in manifesting a desire is first to learn as much as you can, and then take the time to be specific while you imagine what you wish to manifest. I once had a student who worked diligently to manifest a position as a healer, until she learned she needed two more years of work with the teacher before she was ready. You will find it helpful to specify you will manifest only that which accords your highest karma and the highest karmic laws. In this way, you will avoid bringing into your life and the lives of others anything that is not in the best interest of all concerned."

"How can I know the outcome of my desire, my emotional feelings about material wealth, will be in accordance with my highest karma?" Baraja asked.

"As you travel the path you came to Earth to follow and you begin to develop and use your astral faculties, capacities, and attributes, you become more powerful. With power, however, comes the responsibility of using and directing it in a wise manner. Also, the greater the amount of knowledge and understanding you possess about the different energies and how they work, the more responsible you become for using them correctly. There might have been a time during your childhood when you were only in part karmically responsible for the feelings and desires you expressed. Once you become aware of the laws that govern using the different energies, however, you become more responsible for how you use them. You might once have casually wished something would happen to one of your teachers so you wouldn't have to answer her dreaded questions. But knowing what you know now, would you still express the same desire?

"As we discussed in a previous lesson, the subconscious part of your mind cannot reason or think. It merely accepts whatever you give it as a fact, and proceeds to attract to you the energy to bring about what you have allowed it to accept. In the example we just talked about, your subconscious would have had no way of knowing whether you wanted something to happen to your teacher or not, so it would automatically seek to manifest that desire in direct proportion to the amount of energy you put behind your original wish. If something did happen to the teacher as a result of your desire, according to karmic law, you would be partially responsible for that occurrence.

"The astral energies behind emotions, feelings, and desires can be powerful. Therefore, it is important that you not only attempt to conscientiously monitor your astral expressions, but also that you be specific each time you work with psychic energy or your imagination. The more you work with astral energies, the more important this concept will become to you. The greater the ability you possess to use astral energy, the more energy you will be able to use and the more powerful you will become. One of the beneficial uses of this type of power is that you can eventually learn to avoid sending out any negative energy behind your emotions, feelings, and desires. In this way, you will avoid harming yourself and others when your energy ultimately returns to its originating source.

"You can use this power to transform a negative emotional situation into a positive one. People could improve their relationships if they behaved with a little more cooperation, respect, friendship, companionship, and love toward each other.

"You can use this simple but effective technique in your own life. As you become aware of your negative emotions and feelings regarding other people or situations, take the time to find something positive about them. You can learn a beneficial lesson from almost every situation. If you attempt to discover and understand these lessons, you can focus your energies on the positive aspects of any situation, generally overcoming its negative energy's ability to influence your life adversely. The more you concentrate on positive emotions, feelings, and desires, the more you will attune yourself to the positive polarity of all astral or psychic energies. This, in turn, will help improve your emotional state of well-being, as well as your physical and, to some extent, mental health.

"You will also increase your ability to control your emotions, feelings, and desires by working to channel your astral energies in a positive direction. If you like, you can test your astral control faculty by seeing how effective you can be in consciously directing positive energy to any person or situation towards which you feel negative. If you are able to pass this test continually, you will soon discover you can maintain an inner feeling of peace and serenity, even in the most difficult circumstances."

Baraja was fascinated by the concept. "I find it difficult to control my emotions. I seem always to be in conflict with certain people. I feel this is keeping me from achieving certain of my endeavors."

"The exchange of energies on the astral level depends upon the relationship among the individuals. Psychic energy is exchanged in different degrees of quantity and quality, depending on the individuals involved and the type of activity in which they are engaged. For instance, you can give and receive positive, negative, or even neutral astral energies when you share eye-to-eye contact with others, engage in a conversation with them, or even sit quietly in their presence. The same is true when you engage in more intimate encounters such as those involving physical contact or sexual relations. In reality, you tend to become similar in personality to those with whom you associate, therefore, you must choose wisely.

"It might be interesting for you to observe your emotional characteristics and those of your friends and others around you to see if you can determine whether the qualities you see in yourself are truly an inherent part of your own personality or are ones you have acquired from someone else. Once you accept another person's astral energies, you must work with them as you would your own. But after you determine which ones are coming from various outside sources, you do not have to continue accepting them.

"Not only will individuals send you psychic energy you may not want to accept, but also there are always those who will seek to use you as an available source of psychic energy rather than go to the universe to replenish their own depleted supply. If you have an abundance of psychic energy, it is fine to allow the excess you don't need to go out to those who do need it. It is important, though, for you to know that whenever you give energy to others, its rate of vibration will correspond to the state of consciousness you are expressing at the moment. On the other hand, have you ever been involved in a casual or intimate encounter with another person and felt either tired or completely exhausted afterwards? If so, you have consciously or unconsciously allowed the other person to drain your psychic energy supply. Some individuals, particularly if they are negatively polarized, can deplete their psychic energy and your astral body in a short time. Should you know you're going to be around someone like this, you can imagine an extra quantity of psychic energy coming from the astral plane to you or to the situation by using your imagination to pull in the color blue.

"It is generally better to pull more psychic energy from the astral plane directly into your astral body, and then directing it to the circumstances with which you are working. You can also create an imaginary shield around yourself that you can strengthen with a large ball of psychic energy and impregnate it with a strong enough desire that it will discourage anyone from taking your psychic energy. Your shield will be more effective if you reinforce it mentally and manifest its presence into your subconscious when you are working with that level of consciousness. While working with this type of shield, it can also help to use your will to specify in a determined manner that you will not accept any negative energy from anyone or allow anyone to pull energy from your various bodies unless you consciously allow either of these circumstances to occur.

"You will eventually reach the level of consciousness where you will not only be able to accept and dissolve negative energy, but also be able to store up an abundance to share with others. Until you reach this level, you might want to hold onto your own energy supply—particularly when you are talking to or are around negative people—by crossing your right leg over your left. If you close the energy circuit between your thumb and forefinger on each hand or clasp your hands together, you will be able to retain even more of your energy. For those of you who are lefthanded, your polarities may be reversed. In this case, you would cross your left leg over your right. This technique helps you conserve energy and polarize yourself to the positive energies in the universe.

"You can use this and several of the other suggestions I made in this lesson to learn to manifest successfully whatever you desire in the physical. There are few desires that cannot be fulfilled in the physical—as long as what you specify you want is in accordance with your highest karma and the highest karmic laws. I do not recommend that you attempt to energize the desire to grow spiritually, for to do so could possibly speed up your karma to the extent you could no longer function effectively—physically, emotionally, mentally, or spiritually. Instead, strive to achieve balance in every area of your life.

"I would also like to suggest you don't split your energies. The more effectively you are able to focus your psychic energy on one image or desire, the more power you will be able to put behind its manifestation. To prove to yourself that you can cause your desires to manifest, select a relatively easy task first. Later you can begin to work on manifesting greater prosperity, a compatible companion, more fulfilling work, or whatever you wish."

12
Mental Money, Yellow

"The question of why money seems so real, why the bottom line seems to be the most real factor in our lives, comes to this: why have we lost the ability to experience the inner world in as vivid and intense a manner as the outer world? The surprising answer is that the way toward the real inner world is to experience with ever-greater intensity of feeling the pulls and impulses that draw us toward the outer world!."
—Jacob Needleman[2]

Introduction

Yellow creates positive force for clear thinking and for decision making. The comedian Martin Short created a character for the old "Saturday Night Live," Ed Grimley, who, with his pants hiked up to his armpits and his hair spiked in an oh-so-unpunk fashion, used to get himself worked up into a state of near frenzy and comment, " I'm going mental." As we discussed earlier, Ed was in fact "going astral," but many share his misunderstanding.

The power of the mind is beyond our comprehension. We have made extraordinary strides as a society through activating a miniscule portion of the brain and the mind. Activating MoneyForce in our lives requires understanding and using our mental faculties better. The first step in achieving this is to ensure we bring to our conscious awareness only pure, positive energy. In this chapter, we will explore how the power of the mind and controlled mental energy serve the development of our MoneyForce.

How We Relate to Mental Money. Activate the Positive

Nationally renowned psychiatrist, physician, researcher, and lecturer David Hawkins has spent many years developing a methodology, behavioral kinesiology, for testing and categorizing a wide range of human consciousness. Kinesiology is a well-recognized tool in the field of holistic medicine. Its premise is that a mind-body connection exists, and we can measure this connection through a simple test that determines whether exposure to a specific substance strengthens or weakens a subject. The test subject extends his arm and the tester places two fingers on the wrist. The tester then exposes the subject to a specific substance and asks the subject to resist downward pressure on his arm. Agents that strengthen are considered positive, whereas those that weaken are not positive.

Behavioral kinesiology takes the thesis a step further. It states that we can determine if any thought is positive or negative or, to state that in another way, true or false. In his book, Power vs. Force,[26] Hawkins relates using studies in non-Newtonian mathematics and Chaos Theory to prove the existence of powerful attractor fields that, in large part, determine human consciousness and physical order.

We can measure this field through his testing method and assign a calibration from one to one thousand, based upon the logarithmic scale of the respective fields. The range of one to six hundred represents the ordinary—non-enlightened—consciousness. Because the numbers represent the logarithm (base 10) of the attractor field power, an increase from one hundred to two hundred is not twice the size but is two hundred to the tenth power, making small numeric increases quite dramatic.

Hawkins believes the entire history of civilization is the story of the interaction of these fields, which contain the full potential of consciousness itself. Hawkins' measurement of the following fields appears to represent a modified seven deadly sins:

Map of Consciousness

Level	Field
20	Shame
30	Guilt
50	Apathy
75	Grief
100	Fear
125	Desire
150	Anger
175	Pride

Once we rise above this level, positive attractors begin to manifest.

Level	Field
200	Courage
350	Acceptance
400	Reason
500+	Love

We can attribute the development of all consciousness to the conscious choice of aligning with positive attractors over negative attractors. In *Power vs. Force*,[26] Hawkins calls the positive attractors "power" and the negative attractors "force."

All positive teachers throughout history have had a similar message: accentuate the positive and give up the negative. To the extent an individual can keep a positive mental and emotional attitude by attracting positive energies, he will be a healthy, productive member of society. In contrast, those who bring in negative energies experience failure, sadness, and lead incomplete lives.

When we look at a list of the respective strong and weak patterns, who among us would not eagerly choose the former? To name a few: abundant/excessive, admitting/denying, approving/critical, cheerful/manic, determined/stubborn, modest/haughty, and unselfish/selfish.

Hawkins' work claims to be the determinate of truth but is more notable for its integration with the other beliefs we have discussed. It's reassuring to see that different studies can reach such similar conclusions. Spiral Dynamics, Hawkins' map of consciousness, and the traditional Hindu chakra system are remarkably unified. Hawkins' lower levels of consciousness signified by measuring below 200, correlates to Beck's beige MEME and the base chakra. Each relates to basic survival mechanisms. Level 200 corresponds to the solar plexus and can be associated with the blue MEME. Level 500 is similar to the heart chakra signifying love and acceptance, which is represented in the green MEME. Finally the levels of higher consciousness of 600 and above represent the crown chakra and are seen in Spiral Dynamics as manifesting within the yellow and turquoise MEMEs. For all their unique perspectives and approaches, each methodology believes in an evolutionary process of the consciousness through a holarchic hierarchy.

Hawkins' call to accentuate the positive should strike a welcome chord. Positive energy provides the basic building blocks for activating our MoneyForce. In the way Spiral Dynamics uses its color methodology in an arbitrary manner, so does Hawkins in his claim that power is positive, whereas force is negative. As we have discussed, energy, power, and force are three distinct and necessary aspects of Energy that we can use in different ways to achieve the positive results we wish in our lives. What is essential is that we bring only pure, positive energy, power, and force ever into our consciousness.

Hawkins' work supports our belief that pure positive mental thoughts and forms can be a liberating path to physical and spiritual wealth and success, or a debilitating yoke of defeat if those thoughts are negative. He believes our consciousness manifests itself in our lives. If we exude positive energies and faculties, we will attract positive outcomes, including positive financial outcomes, in our lives. In contrast, those who lack positive energy and the necessary abilities and faculties will be poor in other aspects of their lives—poor in relationships, poor in happiness, poor in wealth.

Although I may not be so ready to categorize all poor, especially those in impoverished areas of the world who have little choice in their economic condition, there is some truth to the idea that being poor is as much a condition of consciousness as it is a physical condition. Throughout this book we have reviewed ways to create conditions for generating wealth through the conscious balancing of body, emotions, mind, and soul. There is no question that developing balance in your mental body requires creating positive mental thoughts and forms.

Faculties

One of the primary reasons we use so little of our brains and full mental capabilities is that we do not possess many of the high mental faculties we had during our period of involution. As we lost our connection with the soul and our higher bodies and entered ever more dense vibratory levels and lower forms of consciousness, we gave up many of our higher faculties through misuse, neglect, or outright theft by those who coveted our higher abilities. To regain our proper use of these bodies, it is necessary to reacquire the necessary faculties.

For most of us, obtaining our original faculties is not practical because:

    1.They are difficult to locate and identify, as they may be spread throughout all of existence.

    2.Even if we do locate these faculties, they will be so altered and abused by eons of improper use that to repair and rehabilitate them would require far too much effort. It is easier and better to rebuild them.

Think of faculties as the building blocks of all human activity and consciousness. For example, Michael Phelps has won twenty-eight Olympic medals for swimming, twenty-three of them gold covering a period of five Olympic games. Much of his success is attributed to his unique physiology. He has extremely long arms relative to the length of his legs that provides more strength with less drag in the water. He also possesses great will, determination, focus, and concentration. These, combined with his physical attributes, make him a great champion.

If we want to succeed at any activity in life, or achieve any goal, it is necessary we have the particular faculties required to succeed in our chosen quest. Thomas Edison is considered one of the greatest inventors of all time, yet he failed at countless attempts to develop the incandescent light bulb. He persevered until he finally discovered the correct solution. We attribute his great success to his steadfast determination to succeed.

Faculties encompass a broad area and include capacities and abilities. In developing your ability to find your MoneyForce, it is important to activate and develop the mental faculties that will help you with your work and to learn to consciously coordinate the activities of the three phases of the mind: the subconscious, the superconscious, and the conscious. To do this effectively, you must first begin to understand yourself. Who are you? What are your positive and negative qualities and attributes? Only after you have sought and found the answers to these questions can you truly begin the work of uniting the three different phases of your mind into a harmonious whole to bring about greater balance in your life. To achieve this unity and balance, it might be helpful if you were to understand twelve of the faculties integral to the conscious phase of your mind. The better you understand them, the more effectively you will be able to work with them. Even though each of the twelve functions in a distinctly independent manner, many of them can, in fact, take on the character and perform the functions of the others. They are:

1. Discernment. Though you automatically accept some ideas, concepts, or circumstances because you either know or inwardly feel they are right, others you have to analyze and study before you can decide whether they are accurate and, therefore, acceptable. You need to develop the ability to discern what you can accept intuitively and what you must analyze. Then you can truly comprehend and understand yourself.

2. Receptivity. This involves the mental acceptance of a thought or circumstance once you consider it valid. Some of the information you accept as being accurate will come from your superconscious mind. You will consider valid other ideas or thoughts because they are synonymous with your preconceived conscious or subconscious concepts. You will accept or reject others only after you have used the power of discernment to determine their authenticity.

3. Strength. Strength is the power to accomplish. When it is united with receptivity and discernment, it not only makes your mind stronger, but also enables you to establish the motivating desires necessary to manifest your thoughts.

4. Love. Love is one of the attracting, harmonizing, and uniting faculties of the mind. It is important you strive to attract, harmonize, and unite with what is in accordance with your highest karma and God's highest karmic laws. In this way, you attract those energies that establish the most effective circumstances in your life and in the lives of others.

5. Power. The ability to do, act, or accomplish involves using wisdom, courage, and forcefulness to bring about what you want to manifest. It is the door between the manifest and the unmanifest, the physical form and formless ideas. Strength is the capacity you possess to act, and power is the force you actually use to perform the action. When love and power are combined, a strong drive is established that creates the motivation and momentum necessary to evolve and function effectively.

6. Visualization. Visualization is the power you use to create a picture in your mind that may be present in the physical. The use of your visual faculty alone would result in a daydream, whereas what you visualize with power will ultimately manifest. The visualization faculty is of extreme importance. Without it, we cannot continue to evolve. We would lack the ability to create anything more than what exists already. This faculty is also one through which inspiration flows.

7. Will. Along with your decision-making power, will enables you to determine and carry through with a specific course of action until it is accomplished. Without this faculty, the visualization and power faculties could not unite. Man uses his will to control, direct, and discipline all his other faculties to function together in harmony.

8. Reason. Reason is the mental power by which you reach logical conclusions and achieve intellectual understanding. When reason and visualization are combined, you can express your unformed ideas in a beneficial manner. Reason also enables you to use your will faculty constructively rather than destructively.

9. Order. Order helps you bring about a fixed, definite plan of organization in which you establish one common goal for the mind. When you use this faculty completely, everything has its proper place and functions in the best possible manner according to whatever circumstances are involved in your life. This, then, is one of the faculties that enables you to achieve a state of peace and serenity.

10. Zeal. Zeal provides the intensity that stimulates and gives impetus to a thought or desire. When united with order, it supplies drive to the mind's other faculties and allows you to express enthusiastic and diligent devotion to a cause, ideal, or goal. Zeal exercised without control, however, can develop into fanaticism.

11. Elimination. This faculty allows you to release old ideas and concepts once they have served their purpose and are no longer needed. It is just

as important to eliminate old thoughts, as it is to absorb new ones to meet your continually changing requirements. This particular faculty should be constantly used with love and courage to establish the proper balance between giving up the old and receiving the new. Eliminate thoughts involving fear, hate, or revenge. They are negative characteristics that create tension in your life and in the lives of those with whom you come in contact.

12. Appropriation. This is the faculty through which you are able to acquire all you deserve to receive from the vast resources of the universe. By attuning yourself to the laws of nature, you can continually enrich your life and the lives of others, as long as you do so with pure motives in mind. That which is acquired as a result of covetousness, selfishness, and greed will bring little lasting pleasure and will eventually be lost, whereas abundance—physical, emotional, mental, or spiritual—received by working with the laws of the universe, tends to remain a permanent acquisition. Prosperity and peace of mind are a natural outgrowth of using the appropriation faculty in a positive way.

Maximize Your MoneyForce: Mental Money

Our faculties, used appropriately, are tools for manifesting our desires. Desires are a natural part of our human condition. When we speak of desire here, we refer to positive desires in accordance with our highest karma and the highest karmic laws. It is understood no one will manifest a desire that would harm him or herself, anyone, or any thing. When it comes to manifesting a money desire, be careful about the nature and specifics of the desire and understand that if a desire does not manifest, it is probably because it was not in accordance with our highest karma.

Exercise 5: Manifesting a Desire

Part One:

1. Have firmly in mind what you want to manifest.
2. Be specific. It might even help to make a list of every detail involved

in the entire process of going from imagined desire to manifest result.

3. If you know what you want, but not how to go about getting it, specify that your desire will manifest in a manner that will not be detrimental to anyone or any thing, and that it will manifest in accordance with your highest karma and the highest karmic laws.

Part Two

This portion of the technique may be used as often as you like, but I recommend that you do not work with it for more than five minutes at a time because it requires using psychic energy. If you use too much at any one time, you may tire by temporarily depleting your astral body's energy supply.

1. Sit down, become quiet, lock the energy within your body by crossing your feet and clasping your hands together, then close your eyes.

2. Raise the vibratory level of your physical and astral bodies by inwardly repeating four or five times: I am raising the vibrations of my physical and astral bodies.

3. Imagine and feel the vibrations of these bodies quicken. Attempt to imagine, as vividly as possible, the desire and the end result you want to manifest. If your image isn't clear, repeat the process of raising your physical and astral vibrations once again. In the event you still aren't able to imagine a clear picture, concentrate on the sensory aspects of your desire. Feel what it would be like to have it manifest right in front of you.

4. Transfer your consciousness to the astral plane by imagining several times that your consciousness is functioning on the astral plane. You might also repeat to yourself: "All I am imagining and experiencing at this level of consciousness, I will transfer down through my senses into my physical consciousness."

Begin working with your imagination. Do not think, because thoughts function on the mental plane they are not effective at this level of consciousness. Imagine as clear a picture as possible of the desire you want to manifest. If several steps are involved in the manifestation of your desire, go over these in your imagination in great detail. Be sure to picture yourself with the end result you are working to manifest since you need to work with space on the astral plane. It is important for you to specify and imagine that your desire is manifesting in a precise place or location.

5. There are many colors of psychic energy but for this exercise pull pure psychic energy, which is white, from the astral plane by way of your imagination into the scene you have just created. Use your astral hand, if you like, to compact as much psychic energy as possible into several balls, which you should also direct into the center of your desire. See or feel your desire manifesting in the physical.

6. Lower the vibrations of your astral and physical bodies by repeating several times to yourself: "I am lowering the vibrations of my astral and then my physical body."

7. Transfer your consciousness back to the physical plane by visualizing and saying to yourself once or twice: "I am transferring my consciousness back into my physical body."

8. Uncross your feet and raise your hands slightly upward from the elbows. Allow all of the excess energy you have acquired in your astral and physical bodies to be released out through your fingertips and feet.

9. If you so choose then specify: I will use this excess energy to make my desire manifest more rapidly.

10. When you finish, open your eyes and release your image to the universe, so that its resources might be added to your own to bring about your desire.

Continue to work with this technique until you have manifested your desire. If you determine it is not going to manifest, it may be because the desire is not be in accordance with your highest karma or the highest karmic laws.

13
The Power of Thought

*B*araja was elated and confused. It seemed as though a new world had opened to him in his spiritual practice. He felt the wonderful aspects of bringing the colors into his conscious experience. He was enjoying his time in meditation but often was troubled by how difficult it was to keep his mind from wandering or, worse, become fixated on one particular line of thought until he felt he had little control. Those times when he did bring his mind into a quiet place, he began to see how powerful his thoughts could be and realized the importance of clear thinking. He decided to share his experience at his next lesson.

"I find it difficult to control my thoughts. I have little control, and my mind seems to be continually racing from one thought to another."

Amatamaji knew this was common among those new to meditation. "The mechanism we call mind functions on the three lower planes of existence: the physical, astral, and mental levels. It is the vehicle used to integrate the information gained on the lower planes. As a person functions on the physical plane, observation and perception take place as a result of the activity of the five physical senses and any of the higher senses that are operating. The eyes see objects, form, and light. The ears hear sounds. The skin feels sensations and textures. The tongue tastes flavors. The nose smells aromas and scents.

"The brain processes all this input and makes a composite picture the individual recognizes. It does this by comparing the perceived phenomena with what was perceived in the past. The brain acts as the physical level's mind mechanism as it is the organ through which the mind functions. We use the term "mind" to indicate an abstract concept that encompasses the formation, coordination, organization, and categorization of thoughts and perceptions. The mind functions on the lower planes and gives order to the lower realms' perceptions and their phenomena.

"If a person's perceptions are accurate and they are processed in such a way that their various aspects are carefully categorized, then knowledge of these perceptions can mirror reality or mirror it as closely as is possible on the lower planes.

This entire process depends upon the senses' ability to perceive, the brain's accuracy in processing information, and the mind's categorization ability. If a breakdown occurs at any point, the perceptions will be incorrect. This can have ramifications because thoughts are initiated and acted upon as a result of the observations made initially. The clearer the mental perception, the more accurate the thoughts will be and the more effectively the mind will be able to function.

"Thoughts originate on the mental plane as a result of information gained on that level and on other levels and planes. More thoughts originate as a result of conditions on these planes because most people's consciousness is centered on the physical and astral levels. Impulses from the higher soul planes normally influence thought formation to a much smaller degree. People frequently use mental matter to create an idiosyncratic mental atmosphere, even though they are functioning on the mental plane. In this way, nearly every person creates the mental world that encompasses him. It usually becomes so "real" he is seldom able to see beyond it. This is why many people who function within narrow mental limits fail to expand their minds to their full potential. They function within the concepts, thoughts, and conditions they consider to be fact, regardless of whether they are actually accurate."

"Do my thoughts control my actions?" Baraja asked.

"The mental plane can be divided into a high and a low vibration level," Amatamaji replied. "Thoughts become manifest forms on the low level. The upper level is called the formless or causal level of the mental plane. The causal level contains the realm of higher mind. Here, ideas originate and exist as concepts behind the manifest forms. On the high mental plane, for example, we find the conceptual idea of a triangle as a three-sided geometric shape with angles containing a specific number of degrees. On the low mental plane, however, we find only a specific triangle instead of the idea of the triangle. In this way, the vibration involved in the original concept is lowered to the extent that the triangle takes on a manifest form or shape.

"When a person thinks, he causes thought waves to radiate on the mental plane. These waves appear similar to the ripples a rock causes when it is thrown in a pond. The person's mental body is in the center of the thought ripples that travel in an outward direction. These thought waves normally radiate an enormous distance, as space is no barrier on the mental plane. Higher thoughts travel farther than lower thoughts because the mental matter on the higher levels is more rare and is subject to less resistance than the denser matter through which lower thoughts must pass. A thought wave or mental vibration will convey the character or essential quality of the thought it contains, but not necessarily the same subject matter. A devotional thought, for instance, will elicit devotion in the mind of anyone who attunes himself to that particular thought vibration, but the person transmitting and the one receiving may actually perceive the object of devotion quite differently.

"If we indulge in a thought often enough, and a sufficient amount of mental energy is directed to it, a thought form will be created. This form will exist on the mental plane and will convey a complete idea to the person able to perceive it. Just as one picture is worth a thousand words on the physical plane, so, too, is a single thought form worth a thousand sentences of explanation and description. An individual might spend a long time attempting to clearly define an idea to his listener, but he can rarely be sure the listener is receiving and perceiving the idea in precisely the same manner that he is transmitting it. This lack of clarity does not exist for those who are able to transmit and receive thought forms on the mental plane, because a thought form is more than an explanation of an idea. It is the idea in a manifest form.

"Several factors are involved in the creation of a thought form that clearly and precisely convey the exact idea from the thinker's mind to the mind of the perceiver. I'll list them for you:

1. The quality of the thought vibrations determines the color of the thought form.

2. The nature of the thought determines the shape of the form.

3. The clarity of the thought determines the precision of the form's outline.

4. The strength or energy behind the thought determines the duration or time the form will continue to exist.

5. The entire form will give rise to and will resonate to a particular sound frequency. This sound is an integral part of the thought form.

"Let us, for the purpose of clarification, discuss the thought form and its various characteristics as we would the structure of a sentence. The quality of the thought form is somewhat similar to the subject of the sentence. Qualities such as love, devotion, intellectual activity, etc., cause the form to have a generalized color. Because a pure quality such as love is rarely without a tinge of another, lesser quality such as envy, jealousy, selfishness, or covetousness, the pure quality will nearly always have overtones of other colors along with it.

"The nature of the thought determines the specific shape the form takes. It conveys the activity behind the thought. The type of activity found in thought forms can involve various types of mental energy such as the desire to be protective or the persistence needed to change ourselves for the better. The desire to cling to or the failure to relinquish a person or circumstance, as well as various attitudes such as possessiveness, meanness, and revenge, are other types of energies we find within thought forms. Thought forms or verbs of this nature have a specific shape because they take on the color and convey the nature and quality of the thoughts they contain. Thought forms may be indistinct and delicate, or they may have a clear, definite outline if they contain specific thoughts. A form's distinctness is similar to descriptive words we hear as we speak—they add information that more clearly defines the form. Indecisive or confused thinking will cause a thought form to be vague in shape and color. The more definite the thought, the clearer and sharper the outline of the form and the more distinct its shape will be.

"The length of time a form exists depends on the quantity and quality of the energy it contains. This, in turn, determines the form's ability to maintain its integrity as an aggregate of mental molecules. If a form results from a passing thought, it will soon return to the mental matter from which it came and lose its nature as a form. Its energy will be spent quickly and there will be nothing to hold the form together.

"If, on the other hand, the form was created by an act of will with a reasonable amount of energy behind it, the form may be endowed with a long life that could even outlast the physical life of its creator. Repetitious thoughts can also cause a form to persist for a long time. If each additional thought is compatible in vibration, the added energy will enhance the original thought form instead of creating a new one. Many people do this, because their thoughts tend to follow a similar flow or pattern."

14
Soul Money, Violet

"Money doesn't have any soul but we do and we're the people through
whom money flows and with which money speaks ... And when our spirit is
unleashed, what's unleashed is the prosperity of the soul, of the heart ... and in
that truth, the whole world belongs to you."
—Lynne Twist[27]

Introduction

Violet is the color of pure idealism, dedication, reverence, and true self-realization—the ability to realize who you truly are as a being. It is difficult to speak of money and soul because money has no soul. We each have at least one soul, but money is certainly soulless. Yet money, in its highest and purest form, is expressed through the soul energy that we impart by and through money.

Soul is an often misused and misunderstood word. It has become a sort of brand name for any sort of sincere, heartfelt experience. For some, it is synonymous with a deep, shared experience of a particular ethnic group. For others, it denotes a high level of empathy and compassion, the deepest level of love.

People have a strong sense of propriety when it comes to their soul because it is a word imbued with strong emotions and mental power. A friend, speaking of his new fiancée, told me how lucky he was to have found his "soul mate." When I commented the experience of soul mates was not that common, that it signified a level of commitment to a particular course of spiritual development, and that it was far more likely he had found his "high earth mate," I could see he felt I was criticizing the depth of his love and commitment. That was not at all the case, because a commitment in this life to a high earth mate can be far more extensive and rewarding on all levels than sharing a life with a soul mate in any particular incarnation. Yet we understand that soul is at the root of our meaning and purpose.

In this chapter we will explore the soul of money, the depths from which our innermost essence and purpose spring. We shall learn how balance is the key component in developing your MoneyForce.

How We Relate to Soul Money: Having or Being

Our modern western society is often deplored as having an obsession with material wealth. If this is true, then we are failing in our pursuit. If satisfaction through acquiring physical wealth were an attainable goal, many Americans should have reached satiation long ago. The sad truth is that the consumer society continues on a merry-go-round of consumerism with no relief in sight. Western society requires ever-increasing consumption, just as an addict requires a constant and increasing drug supply to exist.

It should be no surprise that our obsession with possession, with the sense of having, is not providing the deep sense of need and purpose that drives the efforts of humanity. We are "human beings," not "human havings." Until we recognize the primordial root desire of every human to fully experience the essence of being that is our true birthright, we will have no peace, no rest from the continual fear, insecurity, and longing for more that occupies the consciousness of most people on this planet.

In his book, *To Have or To Be*,[28] psychologist Eric Fromm observed:

> "To consume is one form of having, and perhaps the most important one for today's affluent societies. Consuming has ambiguous qualities. It relieves anxiety, because what one has cannot be taken away. But it also requires one to consume ever more, because previous consumption soon loses its satisfactory character. Modern consumers may identify themselves by the formula: I am = what I have and what I consume."

It is ironic that, although we are preoccupied with having, with a sense of possession and control, the reality is that having provides no experience. Think of the central icon of American consumerism, the automobile. There are few other possessions that objectify the American dream. A person who would otherwise be a sensible, caring citizen takes on a new persona once fully ensconced behind the wheel. Our cars serve as alter egos. They represent our innermost desires and insecurities.

I have experienced this. In February 2002 my eighty-four-year-old mother had a stroke. Although the blood-thinning drugs averted any severe damage, the shock to her system drained her will to live and she passed away three months later. As an only child, I was responsible for her care and began a hectic three-month marathon. I drove three hundred miles to the hospital, spent three days, and then drove back for three days with my family and business, and then repeated the process. I was driving a Dodge Durango, and the grief at the impending death of my mother, plus the stress of family and work were taking its toll on my health and well-being. I started to fixate upon the latest top-end BMW—I suppose this was my mid-life crisis. With so much commuting I could find practical reasons for driving a luxury automobile. But the real reason for my desire was a desperate yearning to find some relief from a difficult situation. In my mind, this car was my refuge and retreat.

By the time the lease was over three years later I had come to look at the car with mixed emotions. I appreciated the smooth ride and extraordinary craftsmanship, but I did not like the identity others put on me. I was labeled in a certain way by those who projected their own sense of what it would mean to have that car. I healed from the loss of my mother, recognized I was in the middle of my life, and overcame the emotional challenges that often accompany that milestone. As I did, I determined that nothing in or about that car had anything to do with me. I enjoy outdoor activities and the BMW was ill suited for hauling canoes and camping equipment. At that time we had a home in northern Wisconsin and the Beemer was absolutely useless in the snow.

As I came to understand how my emotional needs were intertwined with a sense of possession or "having" a certain automobile, I realized how often we are held captive by a society that preys on its citizens' emotions by exploiting our weaknesses and promoting "having." True, this may increase sales and serve as an economic engine, but it is ultimately self-defeating, because behind the allure is a lie and deceit. Having something is no substitute for being something. Ultimately, any satisfaction from a possession will be in the sense of being that using the possession provides. Having is perpetuated by conceit and deceit. Being is achieved only through humility and an honest sense of self.

Fromm goes into depth in analyzing these two modes of existence. He begins by noting that the preeminence of having is relatively recent and is primarily a result of our economic system. In pre-modern societies, the economic system was determined by the needs of the individual within the structure of the collective.

In contrast, the need for constant growth to sustain the system drives modern economies. The system does not exist to serve the needs of society. Society exists to fuel the growth of the system. In this modern economy, drives such as egoism, selfishness, and greed, previously considered vices to avoid, are elevated to desirable qualities because they foster growth in the system. Older societies recognized the need to control these human weaknesses, but modern economies conveniently ignore that need and proclaim these once undesirable traits necessary byproducts of the system. In a world where growth defines success, production, and profit, having is elevated to the highest priority. Why produce if not to have, and have more? During the 2000 election George W. Bush addressed a group of supporters at a fundraising activity by saying: "This is an impressive crowd of the haves and have mores. Some people call you the elite, I call you my base."

Fromm posed the question: "In a culture in which the supreme goal is to have and have more, how can there be an alternative between having and being? On the contrary, it would seem that the essence of being is having; that if one has nothing, one is nothing."

Each of the world's great religions is founded on the teachings of men who consistently claim that man will find the essence of life when he turns away from having and embraces being. The gospels resonate with Christ calling on his followers to turn away from material pursuits and search for eternal life. All of the great teachers—Buddha, Lao Tzu, the Prophet Mohammad, etc.—have stated this message in a different way.

In the Christian west, the dichotomy of Christ's message and its practice is evident, yet millions of Christians ignore it. Christianity, as it is practiced in the twenty-first century, bears little resemblance to the early apostolic church with its emphasis on personal mystical experience, or the medieval church, with its focus on following Christ's life through every daily aspect. Why then do the followers of these great teachers find it so difficult to practice what is preached?

We may find the answer in the act of having. When knowledge is treated as a destination rather than a journey, our natural tendency is to become complacent once we believe we've achieved our goal. Although belief can be a powerful force, that strength can be a serious flaw when we treat our faith itself as a possession. "I have faith," then becomes a symbol of attainment, a distinction. Even evangelical Christians, whose faith is based upon an intense personal experience of being "born again," are not exempt from this shortcoming. It often appears the more intense the emotional experience, the more inclined the individual is to believe that further spiritual pursuit is unnecessary, or worse, the search for continued growth may indicate a lack of faith in the act of salvation. In fact, as all religious leaders strongly state, faith is not a possession but a blessing that must be constantly nurtured and supported.

Maximize Your MoneyForce: Soul Money

We experience our soul within the astral body, the heart of the soul. It is easy, then, to understand why we identify the soul with emotion. It is only when our souls are fully awakened in their evolutionary process that a true soul-consciousness emerges, unique and distinct from the soul experience rooted in our astral body and expressed in our mental body. When we are balanced in our other bodies, we provide a suitable environment for our soul work and fertile ground for a soulful experience in this life.

Money takes on its highest level of responsibility and opportunity when we look at it in the context of an emerging soul awakening to its divine essence and purpose. Money can serve those who are committed to achieving their own highest purpose, even though it has no soul. Each person has a birthright unique to them in each life. They have a choice as to the path and actions they follow in either ignoring or rejoicing in the challenge of achieving that unique birthright. Money can be a helpful tool in that realization or a grim chain holding us back by linking us to lower levels of experience and denying us the opportunity to fully experience our life.

Exercise 6: Becoming More Balanced

One of the ways you can begin to become more balanced is to get to know yourself better. The following technique may help you do so. Set aside a brief period of time, which you can spend quietly with yourself.

1. Sit down. Cross your right leg over your left, wrap your right arm over your left, and rest your hands gently on your shoulders in such a way that an outside observer would think you were a compact, oval-shaped sphere. (Note: If you are left-handed, place your left leg and arm over your right as the positive polarity in

your body is generally on the left side instead of the right—as is the case with a right-handed individual.) This will help polarize you to the positive energies coming from without and will close the energy circuits flowing within your body.

2. Close your eyes and imagine there is a soft, transparent shell, or cover, completely surrounding your body. Use your imagination as vividly as possible to become attuned to the thoughts and feelings within your inner self. Remember imagination is used on the astral plane and visualization is used on the mental plane.

3. What do you feel like in the shell you've placed around yourself? Do you feel restricted? Inhibited?

4. Now you will take a good look at yourself and ask yourself some questions. When you do, allow an image, impression, or answer (an honest one) to enter your consciousness. (Later you will need to use the rational, logical processes of your mind to question the answers you've received and ensure you can accept them as accurate.)

> a. What do you see?
> b. How have you felt lately?
> c. Do you accept and love yourself?
> d. Is your self-image a good one?
> e. Are you a happy person most of the time? If not, why?
> f. Are there a number of fears, worries, and problems you need to understand better? If so, what are they?
> g. Are you insecure? Do you feel inadequate? If the answer yes comes to you, ask yourself why.
> h. Are you lonely or are you content when you are alone?
> i. Do you feel confused? Again, if the answer is yes, ask yourself why.
> j. Is there a person or situation you resent or find frustrating? If so, why?
> k. Are you pleased with your life at the present time?

Ask yourself whatever questions you feel are especially pertinent. You may well be surprised at some of the answers you receive. In fact, you may not even like the overall picture you see of yourself right now. Perhaps you will discover that you have been somewhat self-centered, selfish, egotistical, or intolerant lately. Whatever characteristics you see in yourself that you don't like now can be exchanged for ones you would rather have in the future.

5. To begin this process, use your imagination and create a solid, but expandable, storage bin in which you can place all the qualities, difficulties, and inhibitions you want to eliminate from your life. Then, one by one, drop each of your fears, anxieties, and frustrations into your container. When you do this, allow yourself to feel less burdened as you relinquish each situation with which you are dissatisfied. Continue this process until all your difficulties are stored in your storage bin, then seal and lock the container.

6. Allow yourself to experience a new sense of freedom and, as you enjoy this feeling, notice that the soft, transparent shell you placed around yourself has slowly begun to dissolve. Enjoy your freedom for a few moments in much the same way a soaring bird glides easily and without effort from one wind current to another. Just as a bird can experience the freedom of movement, so, too, can you express a sense of freedom, peace, and serenity, now that you have begun to partially detach from many of the difficulties inhibiting your freedom. Begin to feel like a bird in flight.

7. Slowly uncross your legs, then unfold your arms and allow them to glide outward in a flowing motion. Feel as though you have been completely released from your transparent shell. Empty all tension, worries, and difficulties from your container and send them out into the universe, where they can be transformed into pure energy. As you continue opening your arms, allow love, peace, harmony, and balance to flow from the universe into every aspect of your being. Open your arms wide to receive these positive energies. Now slowly allow your hands to fall to your side.

8. Sit quietly for a moment, then begin to relax your entire being by allowing a stream of pure energy to enter the top of your head and flow through your eyes, shoulders, chest, and abdomen, filling every cell, tissue, and organ in your body. Feel this relaxing sensation flow on down through your thighs and out your feet.

9. Once your physical body is relaxed, turn your attention to the nervous system, which exists in your astral body. Let all your negative emotions and nervous tension flow out into the universe, and imagine your entire nervous system being regenerated with a soothing, healing energy.

10. Next, turn your attention toward any mental tension you might feel. Visualize its leaving your mind and flowing out into the universe.

11. Focus your attention on the most positive, serene concept or experience you can bring to mind. Perhaps you will think of the new sense of freedom you have just experienced or of a happy, pleasant time that you were able to share with another person. Let this beautiful feeling of peace and serenity completely engulf every aspect of your being.

12. Open your eyes and go on about your everyday life with a renewed sense of balanced well-being and harmony.

15
The Journey of the Soul

"What is the soul"? Baraja asked as his next lesson started.

"In the beginning," Amatamaji replied, "the monad, spirit, and soul of man existed in a totally blended state of oneness with God. The monad, or Spark of God, is a type of higher consciousness. It is the Spark of God that enables man as we know him not only to have consciousness, but also to be reunited ultimately with God. Spirit, on the other hand, is the energy that varies in quantity and quality and is within each individualized expression of God. Man alone of all the kingdoms—human, animal, vegetable, and mineral—contains the Spark of God, but everything in Creation contains a quantity and quality of Spirit to a greater or lesser degree.

"The soul, one of the vehicles through which consciousness functions, was originally blended with Spirit. Before time began, as we know it, man was not man in the physical sense. He was a monad, spirit, and soul who existed in a blended state of God-consciousness. He functioned as soul in the pure high soul planes along with other souls, all of the original high and low creators, and God, the one absolute Supreme Being. Everything that existed in the beginning consisted of pure positive energy. The negative simply did not exist. Only beauty and perfection existed. The energies that would cause anything else to manifest had not yet been created."

"If the soul is our connection to our true natural state of perfection, why is it so difficult for us to be conscious of it?" Baraja asked.

The wise teacher was quick to respond. "Today perfection would be a refreshingly pleasant state to experience. In those days, however, it was the only state of being the souls had ever experienced. They eventually decided they would like to experience something different. To meet this need, the High God, the original high creators, some of the lesser creators, as well as the low and high lords of flame, mind, and form, blended with one another and used the energy from this blending process to create the lower planes of creation and the different universes, and the cosmic, solar, and planetary systems. The positive and negative polarities involved in the duality of the lower realms were an essential ingredient of the creation process, for without duality, the lower planes could not have been created, nor could they continue to exist.

"Man, as soul, had never experienced the duality of the positive and negative. He was shown the various ways of how dealing with this new aspect of Creation could affect him if he chose to leave his blended state of perfection to experience life in the lower realms. If he chose to make this descent, which some religious teachings erroneously refer to as "the descent or fall of man," he would take on various bodies of increasingly lower vibrations, to exist on the newly created levels of existence. These levels also varied in vibratory frequency, and man would eventually be required to master each of those bodies and levels. In time, he would be able to "return to the Father" by restoring all of the energies within his being to the pure state of perfection and God-consciousness he had known in the beginning.

"Man, as soul, was not expelled from the Garden of Paradise. He chose to leave it of his own accord to experience every aspect of God's Creation. By doing so, he could not only master his various bodies and the different planes of existence, but also many of the different energies in Creation, positive and negative. In this way he could gain more knowledge and wisdom in order to serve God and Creation more effectively. Once man experiences and learns to overcome the negative aspects of his own being and those within Creation, he can more easily assist his fellow man in his attempts to gain control of his physical body, emotions, mind, and soul as he, too, strives to achieve a conscious union with God.

"Once the lower planes of existence were created, all of the souls were given the choice of experiencing the lower levels. Some chose to retain their pure, high state of consciousness. Among these souls, some chose to blend with Spirit rather than Soul and, thus, became members of the angelic kingdom. Angels normally function on the soul planes, but they can come into the lower levels to assist man. Each person, for instance, has a guardian angel that is responsible for watching over, guiding, and protecting him. One of the guardian angels' responsibilities is to help people follow their Divine Path. The more receptive people are, the more effective the guardian angels' energies are in guiding them along the path they are to follow. If angels choose to do so, they may become souls again and become members of the human kingdom.

"Angels can take on any form they choose, though they do not take on the various bodies man does in his involutionary and evolutionary cycles. Some, but not all, have a winged form in which they normally function. The winged appearance angels usually assume is not only indicative of the energies that flow around their bodies, but also symbolizes the freedom a being of higher nature possesses. Just as the birds' wings enable them to soar high above the earth, the winged angelic beings are an ever present reminder to man that it is possible to rise above the lower levels of consciousness to experience the higher, purer levels of Creation.

"Planets and souls alike participate in the involutionary and evolutionary cycles. The soul first takes on a causal, or seed, body in which the essence of its growth and experience is to be stored. The soul's high causal body functions on the high causal plane, which interpenetrates the lower two sub-planes of the soul planes and the three higher sub-planes of the mental plane. To exist on the mental plane, the soul has to take on a mental body. This is the body the soul uses to think, visualize, and use the mind's processes, and to eventually master the use of mental energy.

"The next body the soul acquires in the involutionary process is the astral body, which exists and functions on the astral plane. Emotions, feelings, and desires, the use of the imagination, and mastery of the emotional, psychic, or astral energies occur while the soul is functioning in an astral body. The astral body is often called the seat of the soul, for this is the body the soul frequently functions in during the latter part of this evolutionary cycle, when it wishes to be cognizant of its experiences on the lower realms. The densest body in vibration in all of Creation is the physical body. This is true not only of the physical body the soul takes on, but also of the physical body a planet, like Earth, has. Once each soul and planet has acquired a physical body, the evolutionary cycle for both begins and the long, gradual process of refining and purifying the dense energies of which they consist is set into motion.

"After the soul has decided to involute into the lower planes and take on the various bodies that are able to function on those levels, the soul becomes almost dormant. It will awaken from this stage only after its physical, astral, and mental bodies have participated in the evolutionary process by incarnating time and time again until they evolve to the extent they can send the soul those energies it needs to be fully reawakened. It is interesting to note that at no time during the soul's evolutionary journey does it enter any kingdom other than the human kingdom. Each of the lower kingdoms—animal, vegetable, and mineral—were created for the express purpose of helping the soul evolve. Man can be animal-like in nature, even though he has never been a member of the animal kingdom, at any stage of the evolutionary process. He can be primitive, self-centered, selfish, and greedy.

"In one of the earlier stages of his development, man has to learn to gain dominion over the animal kingdom. Later in a more refined growth stage, he has to gain dominion over the animal-like characteristics of his own lower nature. Just as man evolves, so, too, the lower kingdoms evolve. All animals are not animalistic. Some have evolved to the extent that they are able to manifest the higher qualities of love, kindness, and caring. Animals able to do this are usually not only more evolved, but also they tend to have the highest vibrations within their kingdom. The same is true of the vibrations found within man's various bodies.

"Man evolves ever closer to the higher realms of consciousness, and the energies within his bodies become less dense, more refined, and higher in vibration as he works to master each of his lower bodies and the levels on which those bodies function. With persistent effort and adequate guidance and supervision, man can eventually achieve mastery over himself and the lower levels and achieve the high state of God-consciousness. As long as man lives in the lower realms, though, even if he is a more evolved being who has come to a lower planet on a lower level to help his fellow man, he will be subjected to and have to deal with the denser vibrations and positive as well as negative energies that are a part of those levels.

"Once the soul begins the evolutionary journey, it has much work to do. The soul, you will remember, entered a dormant stage and its physical, astral, and mental bodies must now begin the process of learning self-control. Each of the lower bodies, in turn, must be mastered as well as each of the lower planes—physical, astral, and mental. During this time the soul is completely dormant. It has no soul-awareness. Neither the monad nor the spirit sends energies to the soul at this point in its evolution, because the dormant soul is unable to accept and work with these energies.

"In its dormant state, the soul is also unable to send any soul energies to its lower bodies. This is unfortunate, as the lower bodies could evolve much more quickly if they could receive and work with the higher soul energies. As it is, man is usually ignorant of his soul. He incarnates time and time again, sometimes on physical planets, at times on astral planets, and then again on mental planets while he works to gain control of and develop his lower bodies. He functions within the reincarnation cycle at this time, for until he has mastered his physical, astral, and mental bodies to some extent and mastered the corresponding planes, he has no choice but to reincarnate and learn the lessons involved in mastering the lower levels.

"The dormant soul is not able to exercise control over its lower bodies. The individual must eventually learn to control his own lower bodies. By the time he has mastered the physical, astral, and mental planes and has evolved beyond the reincarnation cycle, the soul no longer has to incarnate on the lower levels. The soul can, however, choose to do so to evolve to and master the higher soul planes, because this is easier to achieve while the individual is functioning on the physical, astral, mental, and soul planes. During the time the soul's lower bodies are still in the reincarnation cycle, they can learn the minimum required to evolve beyond the cycle or they can make great strides forward in their growth and development. The efforts they make will determine the results they achieve.

"As a person develops his physical, astral, and mental bodies during the latter stages of the reincarnation cycle, he eventually begins to seek answers to questions, answers he can find only through the knowledge, understanding, and wisdom that exist within the soul planes. Not long after this happens, his physical, astral, and mental bodies also begin to send the soul the stimulating energies it needs if it, too, is to participate in the evolutionary process. When the soul begins to awaken, the person can become aware in the physical that he not only has a physical, astral, and mental body, but that he also has a soul body.

"Regardless of whether the person is consciously aware of the spiritual realms at this time, she will become cognizant of them sooner or later. When she does, she will ultimately discover that she is Soul. She will recognize that her physical, astral, and mental bodies are vehicles she has developed so that her soul can, in time, function through them when it wishes as it participates in the process of evolving in its own right. Prior to the time the soul has been awake, however, the individual would rarely, if ever, either be cognizant of his soul or able to get in touch with it. The person's physical, astral, and mental bodies must first generate the necessary energy and send it to the soul, in order that the soul is receptive and can attune to its lower bodies."

Amatamaji glanced at the setting sun. Its warm glow radiated light and energy, much like her students. But it was getting late and time was drawing short. With a kind smile, she sent them on their way. She was pleased with their progress and proud of how far they had come. Though she was always reluctant to see them leave, she knew that like the sun, they would return again—bright, shining, and full of promise in the new day.

16
Money in Balance

*"Happiness is not a matter of intensity but of balance, order, rhythm
and harmony."*
—Thomas Merton

In this chapter we will explore some practical exercises that reinforce the integration of your MoneyForce into your life. Here you will find additional tools to help bring to life all of the ideas and images that have been presented. It is sometimes said that "practice makes perfect," but that is not true. Practice makes permanent. If you wish to have perfection in your life, you must practice that perfection. Success in any endeavor does not spring magically from some wistful desire. Anyone who has ever achieved a high level of success in their chosen field will agree that persistent, diligent practice at a high level is the foundation for that success.

Money is the means only to a much higher end. Finding your MoneyForce may help you achieve your monetary goals. It will most definitely provide a sound foundation for achieving your highest life goals.

Earlier we presented a simple technique for meditation. We encourage those who are experienced with meditation to practice the form with which you feel comfortable. What is important is not the type of meditation, but finding a quiet place within where thoughts can be stilled and conditions for spiritual growth intensified. As you begin your practice sessions for finding your MoneyForce, start with a daily period of fifteen to twenty minutes.

We also reviewed an exercise for making vows. We make vows to prepare us for further development and to dissolve the blocks in our unconscious and subconscious minds that hinder finding our MoneyForce. Remember to repeat the karmic clause before beginning your vows:

"All of the following vows are to be done in accordance with my conscious choice, my conscious will, the will of pure God and the highest karmic laws."

Any vow made with this stipulation will be positive and will serve to be beneficial to you or anyone with whom you come in contact. Any vow that you make that is not under the energies of this primary vow will automatically be dissolved and will be null and void.

Following your daily period of quiet meditation silently make any or all of the vows contained in the exercise, or say them quietly to yourself. When you are comfortable with meditating, you can begin a series of three exercises designed to bring your different bodies into balance:

1. Aligning and Blending the Bodies
2. Facilitating Flow with the Arc of Harmony
3. Bringing in the Colors

Aligning and Blending the Bodies

This exercise will help you form a connection through which you can integrate the physical, astral, mental, and soul bodies. They can then share information, energy, and insights. They begin to work together as one harmonious being. It is important to remember that using the imagination takes place in the astral body and visualizing takes place in the mental body.

Exercise 7

1. Sit or lay flat with your spine in alignment with your head. Relax. Close your eyes and imagine or visualize yourself standing, looking to the front. Your consciousness is in your physical body.

2. See your soul body, which will look like you, but pale violet in color, standing nine feet in front of your physical body, facing in the same direction. You will be looking at the back of your soul body nine feet in front of you, as if you were standing in a line.

3. See your mental body standing about three feet behind your soul body, facing in the same direction. Your mental body will look like you look except that it is golden or pale yellow.

4. See your astral body standing about three feet behind your mental body, facing in the same direction. Your astral body will look like you except it is pale blue. Your consciousness is still in your physical body.

5. Walk with your physical body into your astral body. Walk through it and blend with it matching noses, navels, knees, toes, and backbone. This matching works to help align your bodies. Pause with your consciousness in your physical body, blending with your astral body. Energies will start flowing clockwise and spin from body to body. This will look like lots of lights or stars. This spinning is the actual blending of the bodies.

The rest of the technique is simply an alignment process. Attune to these blending energies. Experience your astral body in whatever way is right for you. You may want to ask your astral body questions such as: Is there anything you feel I should know? Is there anything I can do to help us be more harmonious? Are you happy with the way we have been living this life? What could I do to make you more comfortable?

You may find your astral body has many things to tell you. You may also find your astral body to be uncooperative, angry, or needing discipline. Communicate with your astral body in whatever way is appropriate for you. Don't forget your astral body will communicate through feelings and emotion. Try to establish a positive relationship with your astral body. Begin to work together. Remember your bodies are a part of your self.

6. After you have experienced your astral body as much as you can at this time, walk into and blend with your mental body, taking both your physical and astral body with you. Match your bodies at their noses, navels, knees, toes, and spines. Attune to the blending energies as you did with your astral body. Experience your mental body. Remember that your mental body does not express feelings and emotion, but uses logic and reason to communicate. You may want to ask your mental body questions such as: What do you think you should tell me? Do you have any information that would be helpful to us? Is there a specific faculty or phase of mind that would be most beneficial for us to begin to work with? Try to establish a positive relationship with your mental body.

7. After you have experienced your mental body to a certain extent, walk into and blend with your soul body. Match noses, navels, knees, toes, and spine. Attune to the blending energies. Experience your soul body as you did your other bodies. It might be more helpful to communicate regarding your spiritual growth and working harmoniously with all of your bodies. If your soul body is newly out of the reincarnation cycle, it is especially important that you send it lots of love. That is a difficult time for the soul and it often feels insecure and inferior to other souls it sees working with energies. No matter where you are in your spiritual development, sending love to your bodies is an excellent way to begin and maintain a positive relationship. Even those bodies that need to be disciplined can benefit from love.

8. When you finish, you may need to transfer your consciousness back to the physical plane two or three times. Once your bodies are aligned, you can coordinate their different energies by reinforcing your arc of harmony.

Facilitating Flow with the Arc of H armony

The arc of harmony technique is used to bring about a more permanent and harmonious blending of the physical, astral, mental, causal, and soul bodies. You will be able to bring more of the higher energies of your individuality into your personality by using this technique. Your personality, sometimes also referred to as your lower bodies, includes your physical, astral, and mental bodies. Your individuality includes your causal, soul, and spirit bodies, and your monad. You will also be able to bring about a greater state of peace, harmony, and balance in all areas of your life by using the arc of harmony technique, because you will be able to bring the purer energies of the higher planes into your various bodies more effectively.

Prior to this, you may have had access to some of the highest energies in all of Creation. If the energy centers and chakras in your different bodies weren't aligned or were blocked, however, the energies could not flow in, through, and out of your bodies in the proper manner. Once aligned, the arc of harmony makes a connecting link between the bodies, and information and energies received by any of the bodies is pushed up and down and shared by all bodies. As you receive information from various sources on the different levels, the arc of harmony can help you filter and share it to the benefit of all of your bodies.

Exercise 8

1. Find a quiet place where you will not be disturbed. Sit or lie down with your head aligned with your spine. Leave your legs uncrossed and your arms resting comfortably on your legs or at your side. Imagine, or visualize and see your astral, mental, and soul bodies becoming perfectly aligned with your physical body.

2. If you have been feeling negative, bring your bodies in toward the center of your physical body from the left. If you have been overly positive, bring them in toward the center from the right. If you are left-handed and your polarities are reversed, you will need to pull your negative bodies in from the right and your overly positive bodies in from the left. Have you been feeling down or depressed? Pull your bodies up so that your astral, mental, and soul body heads are even with your physical head. Have you gotten angry lately? Pull your astral, mental, and soul bodies down about six inches so they can be aligned with your physical body again.

3. Once you have aligned all of your bodies, transfer your consciousness to the high astral plane and begin to imagine a blue arc of harmony connecting your base, or root center, with your solar plexus center. The arc you are going to create will look like a half-circle on the right, or electric, side of your body. If you are left-handed and your polarities are reversed, create the arc on the left side of your body. The arc of harmony on this level will help unite and blend your physical and astral bodies. The energies on these levels will then flow more freely through your physical and astral bodies. You are in the process of bringing about a more permanent alignment of the two bodies.

4. When you feel confident that you have done a good job of constructing the arc of harmony between your physical and astral bodies, transfer your consciousness to the high mental plane. You will need to think or visualize a gold arc of harmony connecting your solar plexus center with your throat center. This arc, which you will create as a half-circle on the right side of your body, will help blend your astral and mental bodies. If your polarities are reversed, it will be created on your left side. Energies from these levels will then move more freely between these bodies.

5. After you have completed the arc of harmony between your astral and mental bodies, transfer your consciousness to the proper soul plane.

6. Now that your consciousness is centered on the proper soul plane, create a violet arc of harmony between your throat center and your crown chakra on the right side of your body, or on the left side of your body if your polarities are reversed. This will help blend and unite your mental and soul bodies in a more harmonious union. Energies from the lower and higher levels will then flow through your physical, astral, mental, causal, and soul bodies more effectively. When you have finished working with this higher arc, transfer your consciousness back to the physical.

7. Once you have familiarized yourself with this technique, you should be able to create the arc of harmony between all of your different bodies in approximately five minutes. It will be helpful to work with this technique at least once if not twice a day for three to four weeks. At the end of that time, the arc of harmony you have created to unite your various bodies should be fairly permanent, and you will just need to reinforce it from time to time.

With your bodies in alignment and your arc of harmony strong, you can now use the positive, powerful energies the colors contain.

Bringing in the Colors

Use the bringing in the colors technique daily to cleanse, balance, and energize your physical, astral, mental, and soul bodies. Sickness or illness is sometimes due to lack of color, excess color, or impure color. Viruses and bacteria both contain impure colors. Although physical illness must be treated by physical means such as consulting a medical doctor, working with the colors can be used as an adjunct to help the bodies restore and maintain a proper balance.

You will use visualization or your imagination to bring in the colors, in the following order:

Pink
Red
Blue
Orange

Yellow
Metallic gold
Green
Blue
Indigo
Violet
Magenta

Notice you will use blue twice. Use blue the first time after red because red is a strong color and the blue energy calms and balances it.

You may also wish to bring in other colors such as rose and peach, which help bring in energies for self-love and feelings of security. You may bring in a small amount of pale purple, but only occasionally. An excess of purple can cause an imbalance. It is better for a student on the higher path to use violet, because violet has a more balancing effect on all of the bodies—including the physical body—and because it is higher in vibration than purple.

You will notice we use yellow and metallic gold. Yellow helps work with the pure knowledge aspect, logic and intellect, but it does not have the expanding aspect of gold. After five or six months of working with pure yellow, you may also work with metallic gold. Because gold has an ever-expanding quality, it will help you increase and use the knowledge you have already absorbed and learned.

Exercise 9

1. Sit erect, legs uncrossed. Relax.

2. Align your astral, mental, and soul bodies with your physical body using the aligning technique.

3. Say to yourself: "Each of my bodies will receive these colors in a balanced manner." You will feel and see each color coming into your bodies one at a time. Feel and see the colors to be pure and pale. Never visualize muddy, dirty colors entering your bodies.

4. Starting at the top of your head, bring the colors in one at a time, in the order listed.

5. Allow each color to flood your entire being, penetrating every organ, tissue, and cell.

Beginning at the top of your head imagine, or visualize, the color as a ball moving down into your face, neck, shoulders chest, stomach, hips, thighs, calves and leaving through your feet. As the color moves through your bodies, feel and see any impure or negative energy of that color being pushed out as the new, pure energy comes in and takes its place. Guide the energy by feeling and seeing all of the excess and negative color energy leaving your bodies. Say to yourself: "My bodies will retain only the amount of energy they need for balance, health, and well-being."

6. Dissolve the excess impure or negative color energy that moves out of your bodies by feeling and seeing it getting smaller and smaller, until it disappears back into pure energy.

7. If you feel the need, say to yourself three or four times, or as many times as is necessary: "I am transferring my consciousness back to the physical."

Do the exercises in Aligning and Blending the Bodies, Facilitating Flow with the Arc of Harmony, and Bringing in the Colors every day for at least two weeks. Altogether, they should take no more than twenty to thirty minutes to practice, in addition to your regular meditation time. If you are new to meditation do not meditate more than twenty to thirty minutes a day. Do not attempt to practice these techniques if you are angry or are feeling negative. It is better under those conditions to sit in meditation until the anger or negative feelings have passed.

After two weeks of practice, you should feel a sense of renewal in your life. Your MoneyForce is awakening.

The path we seek to fulfill our highest potential as human beings is open. It leads to a great state of love, peace, and light. We need only have faith and continue integrating our different bodies and levels of awareness in a balanced, loving way. If we do our work and move steadily forward and upward, the end result is inevitable. We are on our way home.

Afterword

*G*od is the only presence and power.

I now blend with this power, strength, love, and wisdom as divine energies flow through me helping me to attune and harmonize with all of nature on our planet.

There is only one divine family and that is composed of all positive beings. I ask that I be able to blend with this divine family as my consciousness becomes more expanded from the increasing amount of energies that are being sent to the earth as an evolving planet.

May God's light flow through me, touching my heart, giving my spark more light, bringing me balance, peace, love, harmony, wisdom and understanding, helping to make me a beacon of light for others to follow, to light their path and to raise the consciousness of all people, the planet, and all it's kingdoms.

Sources

1. Schuon, Frithjof. *The Transcendent Unity of Religions.* Wheaton, Illinois: Theosophical Publishing House, 1993.

2. Needleman, Jacob. *Money and the Meaning of Life.* New York: Doubleday, 1991.

3. Wilber, Ken. *One Taste.* Boston: Shambhala Publications, 1999.

4. Emerson, Ralph Waldo. *"Compensation," Essays.* 4th edition. New York, New York: Houghton Mifflin, 1898.

5. Campbell, Joseph. *The Way of Animal Powers, Historical Atlas of World Mythology vol.1.* London, England: Times Books, 1983.

6. Angell, Norman. *The Story of Money.* New York, New York: Garden City Publishing, 1929.

7. Crawford, Tad. *The Secret Life of Money.* New York, New York: Putnam, 1994.

8. Weatherford, Jack. *The History of Money.* New York: Three Rivers Press, 1997.

9. Davies, Glyn. *A History of Money.* Cardiff, Wales: University of Wales Press, 1994.

10. Lietaer, Bernard and Belgin, Stephen. *Of Human Wealth,* galley ed. Boulder, Colorado: Human Wealth Books, 2005.

11. Aristotle. *The Nichomachean Ethics of Aristotle,* trans. F.H. Peters, M.A. 5th edition. London: Kegan Paul, Trench, Truebner & Co., 1893.

12. Tierney, John. *"What Women Want"* op. ed. *The New York Times,* May 25, 2005.

13. Desmonde, William. *Magic, Myth and Money.* New York, New York: Free Press of Glencoe, 1962.

14. James, Sarah and Torbjorn, Lahti. *The Natural Step for Communities.* Gabriola Island, British Columbia: New Society Publishers, 2004.

15. Smith, Huston. *Forgotten Truth.* New York: HarperCollins, 2002.

16. Beck, Don Edward and Cowen, Christopher C. *Spiral Dynamics.* Hoboken, New Jersey: Blackwell Publishing, 1996.

17. Wilber, Ken. *A Brief History of Everything.* Boston: Shambhala Publications, 2000.

18. Kasser, Tim. *The High Price of Materialism*. Cambridge, Massachusetts: The MIT Press, 2003

19. Hawken, Paul and Lovins, Amory and Lovins, L. Hunter. *Natural Capitalism*. New York, New York: Little Brown, 1999.

20. Hill, Napoleon . *Think and Grow Rich*. New York: Fawcett Books,1960.

21. Hill, Napoleon and Stone, Clement. *Success Through a Positive Attitude*. New York: Simon and Shuster, 1978.

22. Carnegie, Dale. *How to Win Friends and Influence People*. New York: Simon and Shuster, 1936

23. Tawney, R. H. *Religion and the Rise of Capitalism*. New York: Harcourt, Brace & Co,1926.

24. Yablonsky, Lewis. *The Emotional Meaning of Money*. New York: Gardner Press, 1991.

25. Gurney, Kathleen. *Your Money Personality*. Los Angeles: Financial Psychology Corporation, 1988.

26. Hawkins, David. *Power vs. Force*. Sedona, Arizona: Veritas Publishing, 1998.

27. Twist, Lynn. *The Soul of Money*. New York: W.H. Norton, 2003.

28. Fromm, Eric. *To Have or To Be*. New York: Continuum, 2002.

Other Sources

Buchan, James. *Frozen Desire*. New York, New York: Farrar Straus Giroux, 1997.

Kahler, Rick and Fox, Kathleen. *Conscious Finance*. Rapid City, South Dakota: FoxCraft, 2005.

Lietaer, Bernard. *The Future of Money*. London: Random House, 2001.

Scarre, Chris General Editor. *The Times Atlas of Archaeology*. London: Times Books, 1988.